The Rita Nitz Story

The Elmer H. Johnson and Carol Holmes Johnson Series in Criminology

Larry L. Franklin

The Rita Nitz Story:
A Life Without Parole

Southern Illinois University Press
Carbondale

Copyright © 2005 by the Board of Trustees,
Southern Illinois University
All rights reserved
Printed in the United States of America
08 07 06 05   4 3 2 1

Library of Congress Cataloging-in-Publication Data
Franklin, Larry L., date.
   The Rita Nitz story : a life without parole / Larry L. Franklin.
       p. cm. — (The Elmer H. Johnson and Carol Holmes
   Johnson series in criminology)
   Includes bibliographical references.
   1. Nitz, Rita Brookmyer. 2. Nitz, Rita Brookmyer—Trials,
   litigation, etc. 3. Women prisoners—Illinois—Biography.
   4. Trials (Murder)—Illinois. 5. Murder—Illinois. 6. False
   imprisonment—Illinois. 7. Abused women—Illinois—
   Biography. I. Title.
   HV9468.F73 2005
   364.152'3'092—dc22   2005006888
   ISBN 0-8093-2665-5 (cloth : alk. paper)

Printed on recycled paper. ♻

The paper used in this publication meets the minimum requirements of American National Standard for Information Sciences—Permanence of Paper for Printed Library Materials, ANSI Z39.48-1992. ∞

*For Janet Coffman and Elizabeth Klaver and Lisa Knopp
with my love and gratitude*

Contents

List of Illustrations ix
Preface xi
Acknowledgments xv
Author's Note xvii

Part One. **Visit Room**
  1. "You're the only one who has listened to my story" 3
  2. Cobras and Pit Bulls 9
  3. Concrete Walls and Metal Pipes 19
  4. Darkness Crowds the Sunrise 25

Part Two. **Trial**
  5. Bibles and Crossword Puzzles 33
  6. Robin in a Cage 39
  7. Apples and Oranges 44
  8. Progress Cemetery 54
  9. Cops, Cigarettes, and Black Coffee 59
  10. "Sometimes she called me Sis" 66
  11. Washed Away by an April Rain 80
  12. Stains, Residue, and Blood Splatters 85
  13. Stool Pigeon, Squealer, and Snitch 95
  14. Trogette 100
  15. Victim or Murderer? 105
  16. Separate the Wheat from the Chaff 116
  17. Citizens of Massac County 123

Part Three. **Truth**
  18. In a Paper Sack Next to the Water 129
  19. Photographs, Dope, and Queers 135
  20. "Some like to eat, I like to fight" 139
  21. A Secret Map 148
  22. "Do we have a problem?" 153
  23. Pieces of Floating Cork 159
  24. Left in Chains 165

Epilogue 171

Appendix: Inmate Status of Rita and Richard Nitz 177
Sources 181

Illustrations

Following page 84

Rita, age two, with her two older brothers
School photo of Rita, age eleven
Rita in 1996
A 1997 photo sent to Rita's father
Rita in 1999
Rita and her two training dogs
Richard Nitz
Michael Miley
Dwight Correctional Center

Preface

I hung up the telephone and waited for my feelings to catch up with what I had said. After telling a woman that I would go with her to dig for a head buried some fourteen years before, I questioned my sanity. The head belonged to Michael Miley, a gay man whose headless body was found in a burnt-out abandoned car near Progress Cemetery, just east of Carbondale, Illinois, in April 1988. A local mechanic named Richard Nitz and his former wife, Rita, were accused of the crime, and ultimately each was sent to prison. For the previous three years, I had visited Rita at the Dwight Correctional Center, where she is serving a life sentence. I had interviewed her several times for a book and, along the way, questioned her guilt. It was Rita who put me in touch with a former inmate at Dwight whom I'll call "Maggie."

Maggie shared a cell with Rita at the Williamson County Jail in 1988 and, a decade later, served two years at the Dwight Correctional Center. At Rita's suggestion, I called her, expecting to obtain information about women's prisons that might be useful to my book. Instead, Maggie suggested we search for the head.

I called a police officer whose advice I had sought before, telling him that a former inmate claimed to have a map that showed the location of the head and asking him what to do. Secretly I hoped that he would go with me, but he said that Maggie could be lying and that I wouldn't get into trouble looking for a head. "You'll be fine," he said. "But if you find something, report it immediately."

We talked about the possibility that finding the head might be the only way for Rita to clear her name. If the head had only a couple of bullet holes and not trauma caused by a blunt object, then the testimony that had put Rita behind bars would be proved false.

After the phone conversations, I spent the next two days preparing for the search. There was no room for error. In case of rough terrain, I would take my four-wheel-drive pickup; in case we found the head or needed help, I would take my cell phone; in case we found the head and wanted to prove it was intact, I would take my camera; and of course, I needed a shovel.

Before I left the house, I threw a shovel into the back of my pickup. The shovel had belonged to my grandfather, a man who had helped raise me and whom I called Pop. I could not help but wonder what Pop would say. He would probably choke on a big wad of chewing tobacco as he laughed and said, "My God, what are you doing?" And then he would follow up with, "You'd better be careful."

As his words echoed in my head, I realized just how caught up I had become. Here I was willing to search the boondocks for a buried head with an ex-con I had met over the telephone. The crime was horrendous by any standard but even more so when viewed through the eyes of a rural community during the 1980s. Richard Nitz was accused of battering Miley with a baseball bat, shooting him to death, and then decapitating the body. Rita was charged with helping load the body into the trunk of a car.

The crime occurred just twenty miles east of my home, but when it came to the attention of the public, I had only a passing interest. Thirteen years later, in the course of writing an essay about hate crimes, I looked into written accounts of the trial and visited the Illinois Department of Corrections Web site, where I discovered that Richard had a long list of prior convictions; Rita had none (appendix). Buried within the reams of newspaper clippings was the suggestion that Rita was a battered woman, an idea that made me question whether she, too, might have been a victim. I could not help but wonder whether the truth was hidden beneath the publicity of the crime. My curiosity could be satisfied only by talking with Rita.

In a search of the Internet, I found the Illinois Department of Corrections Web site, which listed the facility where Rita was housed, and learned that all visits required the inmate's approval. After I wrote to Rita three times, asking that I be placed on her visitation list, she agreed. What I found, locked away within the confines of Dwight Correctional Center—a stone-walled prison for women—was a battered woman, one who had been abused her entire life. Since I too had been abused as a child, the initial pull was obvious. We shared a kindred spirit, an unspoken connection, a sympathetic bond, because people who should have loved us instead brought us hell. It is a union more easily felt than explained.

Weeks later, after reading a copy of Rita's trial transcript, her story began to unfold. She was accused not of participating in the murder of Michael Miley but of standing by and witnessing it and then, at the insistence of her abusive husband Richard Nitz, helping lift Miley's body into the trunk of the car. For these acts, she was sentenced to spend her life in prison.

The Dwight Correctional Center is a nearly-five-hour drive from my house; nevertheless I visited Rita every four to six weeks. Between visits, we exchanged two or three letters a month, and on Monday evenings she called me collect.

My friends asked why I spent my winter nights writing, thinking, and sometimes dreaming about Rita Brookmyer Nitz, a woman convicted of first-degree murder. After all, I am in my late fifties and on the downside of life, a time when moments are treasured, when each sinking sun has meaning. Even my family questioned why I would write about someone convicted of such a hideous crime, why I was not concerned about my safety (maybe Rita knew someone outside prison who might harm me), and if I was determined to write about this crime, why did I not write about the true victims, Michael Miley and his family?

The obvious victim in this case was Miley, the young man whose life was snuffed out in such a tragic way. My attention to Rita never was intended to cause additional grief for Miley's family and friends or to tarnish his memory. Still, most murder cases have a host of victims. From the family of the murdered person to the perpetrator with a crazed mind or the inability to make a conscious choice between right and wrong, to the innocent person who is serving time, misery is everywhere.

It was the hopelessness of her plight, the horrific nature of the crime, the inequities between male and female inmates, and my own history of childhood abuse that drew me to her story. Her path was laced with abuse, three troubled marriages, and an inadequate defense that left jury members to speculate whether the verdict might have been decided differently if the attorneys had been reversed. I was moved to tell her story, not to prove her guilt or innocence. Still I hoped the truth would surface.

I began my journey not as a criminologist, an attorney, or someone with a legal background but as a concerned citizen who wanted to discover what had led Rita to such a sorry state. Whether or not Rita was guilty as charged, her sentence was beyond belief, leaving me haunted by the fact that after sixteen years, she is still locked away. Her appeals had been denied; her family and friends had gone away; and I was rendered helpless when she said, "You're the only one who has listened to my story."

Acknowledgments

I gratefully acknowledge the editors, reviewers, and staff at Southern Illinois University Press for choosing to publish my work. I particularly thank Rick Stetter, Cori Conway, Kristine Priddy, Karl Kageff, Wayne Larsen, Peg Kowalczyk, and Barb Martin for their steadfast support.

This book would not have been possible if not for Elizabeth Klaver, Lisa Knopp, and Janet Coffman. While Elizabeth launched my writing career, Lisa taught me how to write and Janet showed me the path to my soul. Their encouragement was without limits.

I thank my friends and coffee shop cronies for their support and my business associates, George Nadaf and Donna Moore, who listened to my story. My heartfelt thanks go to Holli Marshall, my biggest writing fan and friend when the sea was a bit rough.

A large part of this work served as my graduate thesis for the completion of an MFA degree in creative nonfiction at Goucher College. I have the deepest respect and admiration for Patsy Sims, the director of the Goucher program; my mentors Thomas French, Diana Hume George, Lisa Knopp, and Leslie Rubinkowski; and the staff and fellow students whose presence is felt throughout my story. This work was a community effort.

My love and affection go to my wife, Paula, for her support and understanding when my mind was busy processing Rita's story. My work demanded such an emotional cost that I was left empty at times, waiting for my soul to recharge. I appreciate her patience.

Special thanks go to Rita for giving me a glimpse into her life. What greater gift can someone give to a writer than to share her heart, which few have been privileged to see? Thanks to Rita, I see with a broader view and feel with a newfound depth. It is my prayer that this work gives her a future of hope and lasting peace.

Author's Note

This is a work of nonfiction. Except where indicated, all names are real. While some of the descriptive details used to illustrate the courtroom scenes were invented to enhance the narrative flow, all courtroom testimony was taken directly from the trial transcripts. Thirty interviews with Rita Nitz were held at the Dwight Correctional Center in Dwight, Illinois, and except for a single one-hour meeting, each lasted four hours. Since the use of paper, pencils, and recording devices was prohibited, all conversations were recalled and transcribed from memory and later proofread by Rita to ensure accuracy. Telephone calls and letters were exchanged between Rita and myself; a single two-hour visit and two letters comprised my contact with Richard Nitz. Attorney files, the transcripts of the trials of Rita and Richard Nitz, and interviews with Rita's friends and enemies, two prison inmates, and four jury members provided detailed information. In addition, countless articles and books about prison life and my personal knowledge of abuse victims helped explain why Rita lives in a six-by-nine-foot cell.

Part One: **Visit Room**

1 "You're the only one who has listened to my story"

From the outside, the gray stone structure, turned reddish-brown from the wet winter snow, looked like a large castle sitting in the middle of a field due west of Dwight, Illinois. Farming, Donnelly's printing plant, and the prison provided a living for the forty-two hundred residents of Dwight, a rural community seventy-five miles south of Chicago and just off Interstate 55.

On January 11, 2001, thirteen years after the murder of Michael Miley, I sat waiting to visit Rita Brookmyer Nitz at the Dwight Correctional Center, the primary state correctional facility for sixteen hundred adult female offenders. Opened on November 24, 1930, as the Oakdale Reformatory for Women, it was subsequently renamed the Illinois State Reformatory for Women and finally renamed the Dwight Correctional Center in August 1973.

Earlier, while looking through newspaper clippings written some thirteen years before, I saw Rita's photograph. At the time, she looked constrained, dressed in a full-length white dress with short sleeves and a high collar, no makeup, and dark hair that reached the small of her back. Her head tilted downward; her eyes turned aside. She seemed hidden beneath a dress better suited for a high school prom than for a murder trial.

"Your driver's license and Social Security card will be fine," the correctional officer said, pushing a clipboard and pencil my way. I showed my identification and completed the form, which asked the usual questions: name, address, date of birth, history of speeding tickets, whether I had ever been convicted of a felony. The officer was a white, olive-skinned woman with shoulder-length dark hair, dressed in a military green uniform, white shirt, dark tie, and a name tag—Sergeant Creek.

"This is my first time," I said. "You'll have to tell me what to do."

With a slight smile Creek looked past me as she spoke. "You'll need to purchase a debit card from the machine on the wall." A debit card was needed to purchase snacks. And short of an escape plan, it was the most important thing I could bring.

"How does this machine work?" I asked.

Creek eased from behind the counter and walked my way. "You'll get the hang of it. Next time will be a breeze."

A stranger turned my way. "Here, there's some money left on my card," he said, smiling. "I won't be using it. I'm taking my daughter home."

Three letters had been sent to Rita before she agreed to this visit, and in each letter I explained that I had read numerous newspaper articles about her trial and discovered that unlike Richard, she had no record of prior criminal offenses. Maybe she, too, was a victim.

"You'll need to rent a locker for your belongings," Creek said. "It'll cost you two quarters." Next she pointed toward a small room. "Go to the room and wait for an officer."

Minutes later, a male officer arrived, and like the others, he seemed withdrawn. *Was he angry,* I wondered, *or did his job demand a certain detachment?* "Take off your shoes and belt," he said. "Face the wall with your arms extended and your legs apart." His hands touched lightly as he patted down my clothed body for foreign things. Next he examined my belt, checked my feet, and looked inside my shoes. "Put your shoes and belt on and follow me." I walked through a metal detector and stood at a set of glass doors. "When the door opens, move down the hallway," he said. "It'll take you to the visit room." He turned and left.

Click. The door opened to a hallway that led to a large, rectangular room with circular tables and plastic chairs. Standing against the wall like wooden soldiers was a column of vending machines that offered soda, coffee, candy, ice cream bars, popcorn, and sandwiches that, on close examination, appeared to have been cooked in my daughter's Easy-Bake oven. In the front of the room an officer sat at a large desk; I sat down at a small table that wobbled on the uneven floor.

Except for the officer and a middle-aged couple with a small child, two years old at most, the room was empty. The couple appeared to be the child's grandparents, probably here to visit their daughter. Soon, two women appeared in a foyer with a glass front; one very young, the other about forty. *Yes, that's Rita,* I thought. *She's the older one.* Rita hadn't changed that much from an earlier newspaper photograph: about five feet six with a small frame, she looked a good twenty-five pounds lighter than her listed weight of one hundred forty, and her long dark hair had been shortened to just above the shoulder. Rita gazed through the glass and then disappeared behind a set of steel doors that led to a room, I later learned, where inmates were strip-searched before being let out into the visit room.

While waiting, I remembered newspaper stories about a crime that stretched my imagination. It was April 6, 1988, when Richard and Rita Nitz allegedly drove to a parking lot near Crab Orchard Lake, a place where homosexual men met. In the early evening, Richard called Michael Miley a faggot; moments later, Richard wanted him dead. Miley, a small but wiry gay man, followed the Nitzes to their mobile home, where they fought with words. As Miley turned to walk away, Richard Nitz hit him in the back of his head with a baseball bat. Miley fell to the ground. Richard and Rita loaded Miley's unconscious body into the trunk of his car and drove to the Grassy Bottoms, an unkempt field some two miles from the lake. There, Richard shot Michael Miley with a twenty-two-caliber handgun and, to conceal the evidence, decapitated him. Three days later, the body was found by a group of young people on a camping trip; thirteen years later, Miley's head was still missing.

Click. The doors to the visit room opened, and the two women walked my way. The younger one, dressed in a loose-fitting white top and pants that looked like surgical scrubs, moved excitedly toward the child. The other, dressed in a similar top with slender-cut navy-blue pants, walked slowly, as if time were meaningless. I extended my hand. "Rita?" I asked.

"Larry," she answered. Her hand was soft, and her grip was careful.

"Is this table okay?" We looked each other over. Rita's fair skin and dark eyes were well suited for her thick, brown hair that grew quickly in a world without sunshine. Modest freckles and a slender body enabled her to blend into a crowd, while her natural beauty was hardened by slightly crooked teeth and a face that fought the downward pull of sadness.

"Yes, this will be fine," she answered.

"I guess you didn't know what I looked like," I said.

"It wasn't that hard," Rita answered a bit sarcastically. "I was looking for a southern Illinois good old boy, and besides the couple, you're the only one here." She looked around the room. "It hasn't changed that much."

"What do you mean?" I asked.

"Well, the last time I was here was over two and a half years ago, and it still looks the same," Rita said.

Her remark startled me. "Are you saying that you haven't had a visitor in over two and a half years?"

"Yes, that's right," she answered. "That was the last time I saw my parents." Rita explained that her father was in a health institution and her mother was unable to drive.

"What about your family? Don't you have four brothers and one son?"

Her head dropped; her voice softened. "I saw my son about five years ago. My brothers have never visited me. It's been almost thirteen years."

"You haven't had any other visitors for the past thirteen years?"

"Yes, that's right," she answered.

Several seconds passed before she spoke. "What do you want to ask me?"

I pushed myself to move on. "Yes, I do have several questions. According to the newspaper stories, Richard Nitz beat Michael Miley with a baseball bat, shot, and decapitated him. Is that true?"

"I don't know," she said.

"What do you mean?" I questioned. "Didn't you see it?"

Rita leaned forward and spoke slowly. "I wasn't there; I don't know what happened."

My eyes widened. "You're telling me a different story from what I've read."

"Of course I am," Rita said as her speech quickened. "You're going by what you read in the newspapers. I'm telling you the truth."

"You know I have to say this," I said. "Most people in prison claim they're innocent."

Rita bristled. "I don't care whether you believe me or not. What you think isn't going to make any difference in my situation. I'm just telling you the truth."

I struggled for an open mind. "Did Richard kill Michael Miley?"

"I don't know," Rita said forcibly. "If you're asking me whether Richard could have shot and decapitated Michael Miley, I would say yes. He's capable of killing someone. But if you're asking me if he killed Michael Miley, I don't know." Seeing my surprise, she continued. "I'm sorry I'm not giving you the story you expected. I know it would be a lot easier for you if I agreed with what the papers reported. But that's not what happened."

I moved the conversation to prison life. Rita explained that she worked as a bookkeeper in the garment shop, which made uniform shirts, inmate and dietary clothing, hospital gowns, and specialty items. After working from eight a.m. to three p.m., Rita trained dogs for disabled people. "Sometimes I tutor inmates for their GEDs," Rita added. I was not surprised. Rita, according to newspaper stories, made straight A's while enrolled at John A. Logan College, and her letters were well written.

"Still, I think about getting out someday. Maybe someone will come forward and tell the truth." Rita paused. "Without hope, I'd hang myself."

By noon, two hours into our visit, the room filled with visitors and inmates and the air reeked of buttered popcorn cooked in a microwave that sat next to the vending machines.

"Tell me about Richard," I asked. "What was he like?"

Rita told me about *Sybil,* a movie in which the main character had multiple personalities and could change at the drop of a hat. "Richard was like that," she said. "One minute he could be so sweet. The next minute he might be like a madman." She hesitated and then continued. "I guess I should have known when we got married. We had an outdoor wedding at Crab Orchard Lake. When the minister said it's okay to kiss the bride, Richard grabbed me and threw me into the lake." Tears ran to the inside of her cheekbones and disappeared into the corners of her mouth. "His friends loved it," she said.

While pleased by her openness, I wrestled my sadness.

"After we were married, his violent side appeared more often," she said. "Less than a year and a half later, we separated. And then I had to get a restraining order against him."

"Was he abusive?" I asked.

Rita described an incident that occurred several weeks after Richard had moved out of their home. Betty Boyer, a friend of Betty's named Pauline, and Rita were at her trailer when Richard stopped by, knocked on the door, and asked whether he could retrieve some tools that were stored in the back bedroom. He entered the bedroom, according to Rita, while the rest of them sat in the living room. Moments later, after hearing the back door slam shut, she walked down the hallway into the bedroom and found two of Richard's friends standing against the outside wall. More tears flowed as she described how Richard threw her onto the bed and smashed her face into the mattress.

"Betty came down the hallway and saw Richard rape me. She heard Richard tell his friends how much I needed him."

I could not question her tears. They were real. "That's when I got the restraining order," Rita said, raising her voice. "It's public record if you don't believe me. Betty testified that she saw Richard rape me." Rita paused and then continued. "I'd never advise a woman to get a restraining order. It just made Richard furious, and he beat me more often. I'd call the police, but they never did anything."

The more Rita talked, the more her image changed. In the beginning, she appeared hardened, armed with sarcastic remarks propelled against anyone who threatened her privacy. But now the tears softened Rita's face and gave her a more gentle look, with a hint of tenderness. At one forty-five p.m., the guard announced that visiting hours were over. Although we had talked for four hours, it seemed like minutes. We stood and shook hands. "Come back and visit me," she said with a rare smile.

"I'll be back," I said.

I drove down Highway 47, surrounded by farmland and the prison to my back. "You're the only one who has listened to my story," Rita had said. I felt uneasy, as if I were unwillingly cast into the role of Rita's white knight.

2 Cobras and Pit Bulls

A large part of the state's case was to show that in spite of their turbulent relationship, Rita loved Richard and, like any loving wife, stood by her man. That devotion meant that she would do whatever was necessary to please Richard, even to the point of murder. Some of the logic that percolated through that courtroom was shallow yet understandable. After all, what kind of woman would have married Richard Nitz?

Although the defense said that Rita was afraid of Richard and could not escape his grip, she could not comprehend why she stayed with Richard even though she feared him. "I didn't have an identity," Rita told me thirteen years after the trial as she spoke from the Dwight prison. "I was a robot without feelings." To understand her involvement with Richard, the jury needed to understand Rita. Only then could levels of guilt, if any, be determined.

In the 1960s, one social movement followed another—equal rights for African Americans, protests of the Vietnam war, the plight of the poor—accompanied by the assassinations of John Kennedy, Martin Luther

King, and Robert Kennedy. Beneath the unrest, most blue-collar workers were undistracted by social issues and worked hard to earn a living. Rita's father, Galen Brookmyer, was such a man.

Each day, Galen, a well-built man—230 pounds and more than six feet tall—stepped into his eighteen-wheeler and hauled anything from televisions to lumber to machine parts across a web of interstate highways that linked the east and west coasts. Diesel fumes blew from exhaust stacks into the sky, not unlike the spray of a distant whale coming up for air. For twelve to fourteen hours, Galen, wearing blue jeans, a plaid shirt—long-sleeved in the winter and short-sleeved in the summer—a leather belt with a large western buckle, and a cowboy hat, sat alone, listening to Tennessee Ernie Ford sing "Sixteen Tons" or Patsy Cline's "Crazy." At the same time, the occasional voice of a distant trucker filtered through the static on his citizens-band radio. "Hello, good buddy.... Got your ears on? ... 1040, over and out." And yet, when Galen stepped from his cab, he was anything but private. "Dad never met a stranger," Rita said. "When Dad walked into a diner, he was everyone's best friend. They all loved him."

Every two weeks or so, Galen returned to his home, played with his children, made love to his wife, and two days later was gone. Five children, all of whom physically resembled their father, were proof that Galen had been in town. Rita was the lone daughter, surrounded by a quartet of brothers: two younger and two older.

The lonely nights were too much for Rita's mother, Wanda Brookmyer, causing her to slip into a deep depression. Once petite with an eighteen-inch waist, Wanda mushroomed into a five-foot two-inch, two-hundred-pound woman. "Mom spent most of the time in her recliner," Rita said. "She wouldn't get up for a glass of tea. We did everything. The only time Mom moved was to yell or to swing a leather belt at one of us kids."

Rita continued her reflections as we sat in the visit room at the Dwight Correctional Center in February 2001. "I can still remember how Kenny tormented me. He was my oldest brother. Kenny had this robot which he operated with a remote control. He made the robot follow me throughout the house until I was forced into a corner. Even when I locked my bedroom door, Kenny knocked on the walls, letting me know that he was waiting for me."

Some memories still held a freshness. "He kept after me," she complained. "There was the time when I was cleaning the bathroom. Kenny walked in and told me to turn on the tub faucet. 'Now, put your hand under the flow of water. That's how the end of my penis would feel in your hand.'"

"Were there other incidents?" I asked.

Although reluctant, she continued. "Well, there was another time with Kenny's chemistry set."

"Chemistry set?" I asked.

"My parents had bought Kenny a chemistry set, and he was always doing experiments. One time when I was in his room, Kenny showed me a test tube and suggested I put it inside me. 'This is what my penis would feel like inside you.' When I showed my disgust, he suggested that I could put a balloon over it if I wanted."

Over time, she claimed, the harassment grew. "He said he couldn't take it anymore and that he was going to explode if I didn't help him." At the time, Kenny was sixteen, Rita was ten. "I felt sorry for him," Rita said as her face turned red. "I didn't know any better. Kenny pulled down his pants and showed me how to rub his penis so I could relieve his pain. He fondled me and told me what a woman is supposed to do for a man."

Even when Kenny graduated from high school and left home, her troubles continued. On occasion, when he returned with a handful of friends to spend the weekend, Rita presumed, from the look in their eyes, that Kenny had told his friends that they could have their way with her. "His friends kept following me around the house like I was a dog in heat." I could see the fear in her eyes. She continued to speak. "I locked myself in my bedroom, waiting for a chance to run to the bathroom or to the kitchen for a bite of food. They scared the hell out of me."

Rita's mind wandered as she talked about a white dresser with a big mirror that her father had given her. "I can still remember that mirror. I sat in front of it and watched myself for hours. Like Alice and her magic looking glass, I became smaller and smaller until zap, I disappeared. It was like I didn't exist. I wasn't even a person."

At age fifteen, Rita dated Michael Hayward, age twenty-one—a man who seemed to have everything she needed. The thought of an older man being attracted to her, along with the hope of leaving home, turned Michael into a white knight. But after they became engaged, her interest in Michael tapered off. Thoughts of John, a boy she had dated for a couple of years before meeting Michael, grew into meetings in which Rita and John agreed to renew their relationship.

When Rita told Michael that she wanted to end their engagement, he begged her to stay. "He wanted to have sex with me more than anything. He loved me and said that we would never be together again. I felt sorry for him." Weeks later, Rita learned that losing her virginity cost her more than she had imagined; she was pregnant with Michael's baby.

Michael told Wanda that Rita was pregnant and that he wanted to marry her. Wanda, known to bounce between quiet states of depression and all-out rage, unleashed her feelings. "You will marry Michael," Wanda shouted. "I'm not going to have a daughter with a bastard child." When Rita refused, Wanda called the local sheriff and insisted that Michael be charged with the statutory rape of her daughter. The judge agreed not to press charges if Michael and Rita were married. The options were clear: either the pair would marry or Michael would go to prison and Rita would be sent to a home for unwed mothers.

It was October 18, 1975, an unusually cool fall day for northern Indiana, the area where Rita moved with her family after she had lived in southern Illinois for the first fifteen years of her life. A small Pentecostal church with horizontal white siding, stained-glass windows, and a steeple that reached upward some thirty feet was partly filled with family members. The Reverend Faust, a middle-aged man who held a worn Bible, and Michael, dressed in an olive-green suit, white shirt, and dark tie, stood at the altar. Rita, wearing a dark green dress, walked down the aisle. Before reaching the altar, though, she took a hard right and fled through the side door to the parking lot, where John sat in his 1967 Chevy. John's Chevy idled rough, like most 350-horsepower V-8 engines, as he waited to drive off with Rita to Texas, where they planned to marry and start a life together.

Wanda rushed out of the church, caught Rita at the edge of the parking lot, grabbed Rita by her hair and dragged her back to the church where Wanda restated her options: either they marry or Michael goes to prison and Rita goes to a home for unwed mothers. Minutes later, while Rita and Michael resumed the marriage ceremony, John drove away.

Six months passed, and Rita gave birth to their son, Michael Charles Hayward, whom they called Chucky. She cared for Chucky, attended high school, and worked part-time at the local convenience store. According to Rita, Michael's independent ways were just an illusion. "Michael was used to having things his own way, and he went from one job to another. He was like having another child."

She continued her recollections. Several months into their marriage, after Michael lost his job, she asked her mother for financial help. "You made your bed, now sleep in it," was Wanda's response. Finally, Wanda agreed to take care of Chucky until Michael found a job and they were able to rent another apartment. But two months later, when Rita returned to her mother's house, Wanda refused to give up Chucky. She had made arrangements with a couple to adopt him, a couple who had the money necessary to raise a child.

All of Rita's screaming and banging on the front-room door was useless. Wanda was determined to give Chucky away. Days later, Rita and Michael regained custody of their son; two years later, Rita and Wanda spoke again.

"With our busy schedules, Michael and I spent little time together as man and wife. However, he did insist—" Rita stopped as she began to laugh. "He did insist, why I'm not sure, that we have sex on our anniversary and his birthday." Rita was not surprised when, one day, she returned to their apartment and found Michael in bed with their babysitter, who lived in the same complex. "He told me that they weren't having sex, but seeing them both frantically putting their clothes on made me think differently." Five years from the date of their marriage, Michael and Rita were divorced.

On more than one occasion, when we talked about Rita's first marriage, she spoke of Kenny's gift to her. "He gave me a hope chest," Rita said, looking down and away from me. "Inside the box was a large bra. He said this was my hope chest."

"What did Michael say?" I asked.

"Oh, he didn't care," Rita answered. "He didn't care what anyone said or did to me."

"Did something else happen?" I asked, wondering what other secrets she might share.

"Oh, just the time I was raped."

"Would you tell me about it?" I asked.

She paused and then continued. "It happened when we were living in southern Illinois. Michael worked at a local lumber yard." According to Rita, she went to the lumber yard to pick up Michael and was told that he had been called out of town and would not return for several hours. When a fellow worker asked for a ride home, she agreed. After all, she thought, he was a friend of Michael.

"He had me drive over some back roads on the way to his house. Then he asked me to stop. He had to get something before we got to his house. I pulled over. After waiting for a while, I got out of the car to see where he had gone. He came up and pulled me to the ground and raped me."

"What happened next?" I asked.

"I got up and ran to the car and drove off."

"Did you report the rape?" I asked.

"No, I didn't call the police. I told Michael about it, but he didn't believe me. I told my cousins. They went and had a talk with Michael's friend and told him that if anything like this happened again, they would deal with him. They told his wife. Later, I heard that his wife left him."

Rita began a relationship with Floyd Murphy, the brother of the babysitter Rita caught in bed with Michael. She dismissed the coincidence as just another event in her crazy life. At six feet three inches and 220 pounds, with dark hair and ale-colored eyes, Floyd had the physical stature of Rita's father. They were married on June 30, 1982.

Soon she felt his temper, one that exploded after a few drinks. "He beat me when I was pregnant with his child, causing me to lose the baby and suffer internal injuries that required surgery." Rita became agitated; her voice rose. "Then he had the audacity to whine to the judge at our divorce hearing, accusing me of terminating the pregnancy and putting him through emotional duress." She paused and shook her head in disgust. "We were divorced exactly three years from our wedding day. It was the best anniversary present I ever received and yes, a judge gave it to me."

On August 26, 1999, Murphy was convicted of aggravated criminal sexual abuse of a victim under the age of thirteen and predatory criminal sexual assault and was sentenced to fifteen years in the Big Muddy prison. Murphy's profile on the Illinois Department of Correction Web site (www.idoc.state.il.us) lists a tattoo on his right arm that says "Love You Always RJ." *R* and *J* are the initials for Rita Jo.

"Of course you know my third husband. Richard and I were married on October 22, 1986, and I filed for divorce one year later. It was one year of pure hell." Rita described Richard as a man with a Jekyll-Hyde personality; he could woo you or destroy you. The two met during the spring of 1983 at a party and then again, three years later, when she was working at a local convenience food store in Carbondale. At the time, Rita was taking medication for the flu and began feeling dizzy. She told her employer that she was ill and had to go home. Before reaching her car, however, she fell to the ground. It was fate, Rita later thought, that Richard found her lying on the ground, carried her to his car, and took her to the hospital emergency room.

"He was so kind," Rita later said. "I'd never had a man treat me so nice."

That was before she saw his evil side. Rita's mother, Wanda Brookmyer, claimed that Richard could put a spell over people. "He had a way about him. His friends would do anything he said. Rita was scared to death of him. You ought to meet him. You'd see."

In January 1988, after Richard had moved out, a judge issued a restraining order against him. Several times, when he came by the trailer, Rita called the sheriff to report that he was back, and thirty minutes later, a deputy might or might not appear, only to find Richard gone or peeling away as he sped down the road. "The restraining order made matters worse," she said.

She asked her cousin, Larry Brookmyer, and a friend, whom we will call Roy Dulaney, to stay at her trailer for protection. For more than a month, Larry stayed during the daytime and Roy stayed at night. Each testified that Richard frequently came to the trailer, and according to Roy, they kept a bat behind the chair in case Richard's anger broke out.

It was late April of 2001. Rita and I were sitting in the visit room, and as she so often did, Rita held a bottle of Diet Mountain Dew in her right hand and scraped off the label with the fingernails of her left hand, staring at the bottle while she talked.

"There were times when he told me that I just didn't get it," Rita said. "Richard said that I would do what he told me to do. And that I didn't have a choice. I was his piece of property. One time before Miley's death, he even asked me if I'd ever seen a dead person. I asked an attorney to check missing persons. Maybe Richard had killed someone. But the attorney said that Richard was just trying to scare me."

Rita was battered, beaten, blamed, bruised, disgraced, fondled, harassed, raped, restrained, shamed, terrorized, tortured, and violated, all within a run of twenty-nine years. When asked why she stayed with such men, Rita answered, "I thought they would change."

Whatever the reasons, one cannot understand Rita's behavior without a thorough knowledge of battered women. Abuse victims have been programmed differently; they are trapped in a quicksand of violence, and no matter how hard they try, pulling out of the abusive situation is extremely difficult or, in some cases, impossible.

Neil Jacobson and John Gottman, both professors of psychology at the University of Washington and the authors of a 1998 book, *When Men Batter Women: New Insights into Ending Abusive Relationships,* say that men who batter women are like cobras or pit bulls. The cobra silently slithers through the grass before striking its victim, while the pit bull's anger builds and builds until it attacks with a sudden burst, setting its teeth, unwilling to surrender its grip.

After a decade of study, Jacobson and Gottman believe that their classifications provide a better understanding of men who abuse women. "Pit bulls are great guys, until they get into an intimate relationship. O. J. Simpson is a classic pit bull. Pit bulls confine their monstrous behavior to the women they love, acting out of emotional dependence and a fear of abandonment. Pit bulls are the stalkers, the jealous husbands and boyfriends who are charming to everyone except their wives and girlfriends."

Jacobson and Gottman explain cobras differently. "Cobras, on the other hand, are often sociopaths. They are cold and calculating con artists relatively free of the trappings of emotional dependence, but with a high incidence of antisocial and criminal traits and sadistic behavior. Cobras' violence grows out of a pathological need to have their way, to be the boss and make sure that everyone, especially their wives and girlfriends, knows it and acts accordingly."

The histories of cobras and pit bulls are quite different. "Cobras often had violent, traumatic childhoods, criminal records and a personal history of alcohol and drug abuse. Pit bulls, on the other hand, are less likely to have a history of delinquency or criminal behavior, but they are more likely than cobras to have had fathers who battered their mothers."

Contrary to the claims of batterers, their wives rarely do or say anything that would provoke a vicious attack in a nonviolent marriage. There is nothing a wife can say or do to fend off a battering episode. Most often, when a woman tries to end an attack by fleeing, the husband pursues her and intensifies the attack.

Rita's childhood abuse made the transition into abusive marriages seem quite normal. After all, who were the male figures in her life? Rita's father was gone most of the time, leaving Kenny, an abusive older brother, to set the bar.

So we should not wonder why Rita married Richard. Rather, we should be surprised she had the guts to leave him, obtain a restraining order, and call the police, who nevertheless did little to protect her.

It was May 2001. Rita and I sat in the visit room at Dwight Correctional Center during my fourth trip to Dwight, and like before, we were having a four-hour meeting. Added to my visits had been a series of telephone calls and numerous letters from Rita. We had developed a level of trust and understanding, and the questions were easier to ask.

Since it was the middle of the week, only three or four tables were occupied by visitors and inmates. At the front of the gymlike room were two female prison guards dressed in dark green and sitting at a large desk. We were surrounded by rows of vending machines.

For three hours or so, I had been asking questions: some prepared and some off the cuff. My thoughts drifted back to a conversation we had during one of my earlier visits, one that dealt with how Richard treated Rita in front of his friends. Her words were edged into my mind, cold and crisp like a morning frost. "If they wanted a beer and I refused to get it, Richard told them to slap me around a bit." I remembered her comparison of Richard to Floyd Murphy, her second husband. "Floyd was violent, but at least he didn't let anyone else touch me. I respected him for that." Rita had seemingly stopped in the middle of her story, making me wonder if there was more.

As I brought up the past conversation, Rita leaned back from the table. "I see no reason to talk about that," she said.

"Why do you say that?" I asked.

"It's not important. There's no point in discussing it," Rita answered with a frown.

My curiosity grew. I stressed the importance of getting to know her and how anything she shared would be helpful. We sat in silence. Her face tightened.

"It was a Sunday afternoon," she said. "Richard and I were riding our motorcycles in Giant City Park. Richard had picked up some beer. I never drank. Four men on motorcycles pulled up beside us." Rita stopped, looked down, and studied the floor. "Richard invited the four men to join us. It was late afternoon, and the air was chilly. I wanted to go home, but Richard insisted we stay. The four men rode with us as Richard led the group over different trails. Then he suggested that we go to some pond, build a bonfire, and drink some beer. I begged to go home, but he only became more upset." By now, tears ran down her face; her lips quivered; she wrestled her thoughts. "They made a big fire by the pond. Everyone was drinking and smoking pot. I sat away from the group and fought off passes from the other bikers. Richard became more angry." Suspecting what might come next, I reached across the table and held her hand.

"Richard walked over to me, slapped me a few times, and dragged me to the fire and told the men they could have their way. They raped me. All of them."

"I'm so sorry," I said.

"They all got on their bikes and left. Richard left too. I got dressed and found my way back to the main road and went home."

As I left that day I tried to record my thoughts on a handheld recorder while driving down Highway 47. But I couldn't. My mind was unsettled, my voice unsteady. To my right was a worn-down man wrestling a tractor over a freshly plowed field, and just ahead was a hawk circling some road kill. My car bounced once or twice as I crossed a set of tracks. Rita's story had reached deep into my soul, a place where secrets are kept. Secrets that burn like cooked flesh, when I think of someone I wish I had never met. When my brother threw me across some hay, in a barn just east of a white house and next to a machine shed. A place where my brother had his way.

3 Concrete Walls and Metal Pipes

Dust blew across the field that circled the Dwight Correctional Center. The summer day was unusually dry, and the farmers needed a slow rain. What an eerie sight, to see a stone prison that seemingly had flown from another place, another world, and landed in the middle of a bean field in midwestern Illinois. I pulled into the parking lot, stepped from my car, and walked toward the entrance. A security van inched my way. It was 8:54 a.m.; the door opened at nine. I turned slowly and scanned the prison yard. High along the top of a chain-link fence were rows of barbed wire that could gut a fish's belly in a flash.

A man with painted arms and long, black hair pulled back into a ponytail walked my way. "We got a few minutes until nine," he said. "Everything is by the rules."

"Yes, I know what you mean."

"Where did you come from?" he asked in a friendly way.

"Carbondale," I said.

"Whoa," he answered as his eyes widened. "You had quite a trip. I've been coming here one time each week, and I'm getting tired of it. I'm too old for this." He shook his head. "I'm seventy-two. I'll be dead before my wife gets out."

"How long is she in for?" I asked.

He looked down and kicked at the dirt. "Ninety years. She left me for a year and ran around with a younger crowd. She's twenty-three. She got into drugs, and now she's here. Choices, everybody's got choices, and she made the wrong one. If she hadn't left me, she wouldn't be here. Bet she's sorry now."

Click. The door opened. I went to the counter and waited my turn. "I'm here to see Rita Brookmyer Nitz N97463."

An officer dressed in a stiff, pale green short-sleeved shirt checked his computer screen, picked up the receiver, and made a call. He, too, had painted arms. "Bring Rita Nitz down," he said. "She's got a visitor."

I turned and did the usual: purchased a debit card, put my belongings in a locker, and walked to a small room where I took off my belt and shoes and waited to be searched. Next I passed through a metal detector, a hallway, and two doorways before entering the visit room. I picked out a round table with two chairs and sat down.

The man with painted arms chose a table some fifty feet from me, and another man sat to my right. We were the first visitors for the day. Two young female inmates dressed in blue jumpsuits kept busy wiping down tables with soft, wet rags. Rita had told me that inmates in blue jumpsuits were called "intakes": women recently transferred to Dwight but not yet assigned a minimum, medium, or maximum security level. Another intake with still eyes, some six or seven months pregnant, sat next to the officer. She looked no older than sixteen.

The routine was interrupted when two large men and one stout woman, carrying black helmets with plastic masks, entered the visit room. Each wore an orange jumpsuit, a bulletproof vest, freshly polished black shoes, thick gloves, and a belt with canisters and other things hanging from it. Their faces were flushed and showed an air of excitement. With their helmets in place, not a speck of skin was visible. *What would it feel like,* I wondered, *if six of them came into your cell? And these inmates are women. Are they that violent?*

An inmate arrived and disappeared behind a door adjacent to the visit room. *She's probably doing the dance,* I thought. "The dance" is what Rita called the procedure that inmates underwent behind those closed doors. During one of my earlier visits, Rita raised her hands back behind her head and lifted her long hair into the air. "First I lift my hair up and slowly turn around so they can see if I'm hiding any contraband," she said. "It's like I'm dancing at some strip joint. I lift my breasts up and they take a close look. Then I twirl around and bend over and spread the cheeks. And if that's not enough, they take their little flashlights and see if I'm hiding something you know where. They might call in some more guards who take their flashlights and have a look. If they're still uncertain, they take you to the infirmary for a cavity search."

Now, as I waited, I imagined that I was a young man who had come to see Rita as a teenager. After meeting her parents, they tell me to wait in the living room and that she will be right down. The TV is on, and her father and I watch in silence. The rattle of dishes can be heard through the kitchen door. Sandy, her spotted dog, jumps on the sofa and licks my hand. But reality is different; this is the visit room, a place where everything is hard. The chairs and tabletops and legs are hard. The floors are tiled, and the ceiling and walls are stone. Even each word, spoken in a normal tone, is hard and bounces around until it finally dies. I've learned to speak softly and direct each word into the softness of Rita's chest; she sends her words into mine. That's how we talk in the visit room.

How can I understand this place where they cage people? It's a warehouse run by guards who herd inmates into cubicles separated by concrete walls and metal pipes. A psychologist who works in a prison said, "There's only one difference between inmates and prison guards. The prison guards get to go home at night." Are prison guards the brutal stereotype we see in such movies as *Shawshank Redemption*?

Thomas Mott Osborne, Sing Sing's warden in 1914 and a nationally renowned prison reformer, believed that prisoners are treated like wild animals and that the system brutalizes the men and the keepers. To taste the reality of prison, Osborne asked to be housed, clothed, fed, and treated like the inmates. His short experience yielded the expected. "I believe every man in this place hates and detests the system under which he lives," said Osborne. "He hates it even when he gets along without friction. He hates it because he knows it is bad; for it tends to crush slowly but irresistibly the good in himself."

Jack Henry Abbott, an inmate who wrote *In the Belly of the Beast*, openly voiced his hostility for prison guards. "The pigs in the state and federal prisons—especially in the judicial system—treat me so violently," he wrote. "I cannot possibly imagine a time I could ever have anything but the deepest, aching, searing hatred for them. I can't begin to tell you what they do to me. If I were weaker by a hair, they would destroy me."

We should not ignore the words of Abbott, a product of our penal system who could arguably be called "society's child." Abbott, in and out of foster homes from the time he was born, began serving time in the juvenile detention quarters at age nine. By his twelfth birthday, he was at the Utah State Industrial School for Boys. He was released at age eighteen but was incarcerated again six months later at Utah State Penitentiary for "issuing a check against insufficient funds." Three years into his five-year sentence, Abbott killed one inmate and wounded another during a prison fight. At age twenty-six, he escaped from prison, committed robbery, and was captured six weeks later. In 1981 he was released on parole and, six weeks later, stabbed and killed a twenty-two-year-old man. And on a Sunday in February 2002, Abbott hanged himself with a bedsheet and a shoelace. If any attempts were made to rehabilitate Abbott, they failed miserably.

Ted Conover, an investigative journalist who became a recruit in the Albany Training Academy and later a correctional officer at Sing Sing prison, said that little has changed from the nineteenth-century prison guard to today's correctional officer. In his book *NewJack*, Conover says that although guards are feared, some are liked and some are hated, some issue an array of punishments and some issue none, and while some are honest, others are not.

Rita joined me in the visit room and talked about prison guards. "There's some good ones," she said. "Some of the older guards bend over backwards and seem to care. But that's a small percentage." She began to smile. "In the old days, when there were about four hundred inmates, we knew the guard's name, their wife's name, and even the names of their kids. Everybody got along. But it's different now." Her smile disappeared. "Most of the guards, especially the young ones, are on a power trip. They love to make your life miserable. At times, it seems like the prison is being run by a young street gang."

An increasing prison population aggravates the problem. In June 2004, the Illinois Department of Corrections housed 44,379 adult inmates in twenty-seven state prisons at a cost per capita of $22,627 per year. While 94 percent were men and 6 percent women, 28 percent were white, 61 percent black, and 11 percent Hispanic. Seventeen percent were convicted murderers, with five on death row, and like Rita, 1,314 were lifers.

The population of female inmates grew from 1,191 in 1990 to 2,712 in 2002—a 128 percent increase—with a projected increase to 3,493 by the end of 2004. A swift gain in numbers can be attributed in large part to a 270 percent increase in convicted drug offenders over the same period.

In her book *Whores and Thieves of the Worst Kind: A Study of Women, Crime, and Prisons, 1835–2000*, L. Mara Dodge writes, "Women sentenced to prison today are overwhelmingly poor, marginalized and disadvantaged." Dodge says that women are being incarcerated in "historically unprecedented numbers" and attributes this phenomenon to our "draconian criminal justice policies." She argues that the decision to prosecute an act depends as much on the character of the accused, the prejudices of the prosecutor, and the norms of the community as on the act itself.

Ed Garvey, writing for the *Capital Times*, calls the prison system an "immoral growth industry." The growing numbers have resulted in proposed new construction, such as the $100 million women's facility in Illinois' Pembroke Township, which will provide 750 jobs and an annual budget of $54 million. "As long as prisons bring jobs and extra spending money to a community," Garvey says, "it is difficult to imagine local politicians taking a sensible approach to sentencing decisions, not to mention parole." Prisons have become political handouts.

Prison is a home for violent people, the mentally ill—10 to 20 percent of the prison population, according to a recent New York study—and others who hold on to survive. A continuous stream of new prisoners, some chronic drug users and others who long for a taste of tobacco, adds to the list of inmates at Dwight Correctional Center. Without drugs or the pull from a cigarette, violence is as close as a cross word or a surly look. Add this tension to the fact that inmates live in six-by-nine-foot cells with someone they may dislike, and anger smolders like smoke before the fire. "There's a fight every day," Rita said. "It may be a fistfight, or you could be cut with a knife. It happens all the time."

"Have you ever had to fight?" I asked.

"One time," Rita answered. "It wasn't a pretty sight."

Only one fight during thirteen years. I was not surprised. When I see Rita from a distance, she appears indistinguishable, almost ghostlike as she floats silently among the prison population. At times she disappears and moves through the violence untouched. "Sometimes I walk up to a guard or another inmate and they don't see me," Rita said. "It's like I don't exist." But when Rita joins me at the small round table in the visit room, her features take shape; her face adds color; she glows.

4   Darkness Crowds the Sunrise

All the prisoners look the same. Their eyes, filled with troubled yesterdays, reflect the stillness of pond water. My thoughts drift to the shamanistic practice performed some thirty thousand years ago, when ancient tribes believed that if a person suffered a severe trauma, their soul broke away. Even today, as Sandra Ingerman writes in *Soul Retrieval*, psychology recognizes that parts of the self can become separated, leaving the person estranged from his or her essential self. Maybe Rita lost her soul.

At 9:15 a.m., June 21, 2001, I sat in the visit room, waiting to see Rita. After six months, the routine was familiar. Since Rita was late, I wondered whether there was a problem, and while trying to crack a joke, I asked whether she had escaped.

"We don't use that word in here," the guard insisted.

Minutes later, Rita walked through the doors to the visit room. Her face was flushed, sweat-covered, and she looked uneasy.

"Is something wrong?" I asked. She struggled to speak. "Slow down," I said. "Tell me what happened."

"He took a swing at me," she said. "He needs to know that I'll never allow anyone to abuse me again." She looked at me and then to her side.

"What are you talking about?" I asked. "Start from the beginning and tell me what happened."

An inmate, according to Rita, told someone outside the Dwight Correctional Center that a supervisor abused the dogs used in the canine training program for disabled people. The details were unclear. Anyway, the supervisor, hoping to find contraband (any items purchased outside the prison commissary), ordered a shakedown of Rita's cell block. After a box of Q-tips, a brand not sold in the commissary, was found in Rita's cell, she was charged with having contraband and ordered to appear before a disciplinary committee.

The supervisor, having been at Dwight for two or three years, failed to realize that Rita, over her thirteen-year tenure, had purchased different brands of cotton swabs from the commissary. Although Rita explained, he held firm. And when she pushed the issue, he took a swing at her. Rita dodged the blow, fled his office, and an hour later, was in the visit room.

Visiting hours ended, and as I drove home that day, I questioned her reality. *Did the supervisor take a swing at Rita? Could this kind of thing happen over a box of Q-tips? Was I being manipulated?* I have struggled to understand what I call prison country and to open my heart and let the edges of my reality grow. In Rita's world, rights and freedoms are peeled away like layers of onion skin until inmates depend on the guards for life's most basic needs. The guard becomes the parent; the inmate becomes the child.

Two days later I received a telephone call from John Young, a friend of Rita's, who told me that Rita had called and asked him to let me know that she had been placed in segregation.

"What does she expect me to do?" I asked.

"I don't know," John said. "I just know that she couldn't reach you and asked me to call and let you know what's going on."

Communication between an inmate and an outsider is limited to visiting hours, mail, and collect calls from the inmate. But segregation is different. Any exchange between Rita and me had been terminated temporarily. Rita was an outcast, not only from society but also from the prison community.

In July of 2001, just weeks after being released from segregation, Rita told me her story. She had reported the supervisor for taking a swing at her and was placed in segregation, where her thoughts were her only companion. Although she passed a polygraph test four days later, her misery multiplied. She was moved to a different cell block, her job was taken away—a job she had held for ten years—and the dogs she had trained for the canine program were taken from her. She was stripped of everything that gave her purpose; she slid into depression. Fifty lashes across her back side would have been less painful and would have provided an end to her punishment.

"I can't take this anymore," Rita said, as she struggled to speak.

"What can you do?" I asked.

"I can end it all," Rita answered, staring at her soft drink while she peeled away slivers of a Mountain Dew label with her thumbnail.

"What do you mean, end it all?" I asked.

"Just what I said," she argued. "I can end it all."

I leaned forward and chose my words carefully. "Are you talking about killing yourself?"

Rita explained how they had taken everything from her, but they could not tell her when she would die. "It's the only thing I control," she said.

Our conversation was interrupted by a group of people, maybe a dozen or so, being led through the visit room by someone who appeared to be in charge. "Who is that?" I asked.

With an angry look, Rita said, "It's a tour group. They're going to look us over." For a sliver of time—maybe two minutes at most—I was on the other side, a place where outsiders looked us over, even me, with not a direct stare but more of a glance when they thought I was not looking. The uneasiness was sudden, unfamiliar, and unannounced. *Why are they looking at me?* I wondered. My thoughts were swift. *Do they know I'm not an inmate? I'm a visitor. Maybe they think I'm just like the prisoners. No, that's not it. Maybe they think we're at the zoo, but this time I'm in the cage. God, I wish they'd leave.*

The group brushed by our table while the leader talked about the visit room, a place where inmates were rewarded for good behavior.

Rita raised her voice. "They don't reward anyone for good behavior."

Members of the group looked her way. I quickly reached across the table and grabbed her arm.

"Don't say anything," I insisted.

"What more can they do to me?" Rita asked.

"Look what they did last time," I said. Rita stopped and stared at the tabletop. *In the beginning,* I remembered, *I had planned on taking a tour of the prison, hoping to get a close view of the cells, the cafeteria, to smell the air and see their faces. But not anymore.*

The following month, in late summer when the bean fields that surrounded the prison were a golden brown, I made another trip to the visit room. "My father died on the same day you were here last month," Rita said. "They waited until the visiting time was over before they told me. I'm beginning to believe that you're bad luck. Something bad always happens when you come to visit."

"I'm sorry," I said. "You should have called me. I would have come to the funeral and we could have talked." Because of poor health, Rita's father had spent his last few years in a nursing home. Each time his name was mentioned during previous visits, a warmth seemed to flow through her and light the room.

"I didn't go to the funeral," she said. "They wouldn't let me go."

I was amazed by their refusal to let Rita attend her own father's funeral, but I was even more surprised by her outward acceptance of his death and her dilemma.

"You seem to be at peace with things," I said. "But I don't understand why."

Rita smiled slightly. "Yes, I'm more at peace. That happens when you reach a resolve."

"What do you mean?" I asked.

"Well, I know what I need to do, how to do it, and when," Rita said.

"Are you still planning to kill yourself?"

Rita nodded. There was silence. I moved back in my chair and then leaned forward, making certain we made eye contact. "Say something," I insisted. "Are you really serious?"

"Yes, but I'm not going to talk about it," Rita said. "There's nothing more to say."

"What do you mean?" I asked. "You can't leave me like this. What am I supposed to do?"

"Nothing. You don't need to do anything," Rita insisted.

My drive home seemed longer than before. Whether Rita was sharing her feelings with someone she trusted or whether she was using some premeditated strategy to gain my support was unclear. But I decided to assume that Rita was serious and I should act accordingly.

If I told the prison officials about our conversations, they would place her in a cell covered with four-inch-thick pads, isolated from other inmates. Suicide would have been denied, but only for the moment.

Days later, some of my friends offered their thoughts. "You have to tell the prison officials. At least you would remove all responsibility from yourself and you would have saved a life." *They don't understand,* I thought. *How could I deny Rita's last grasp at control?* To understand Rita, I needed to look into the heart of someone who has been a friend of death, who has smelled the lure of its aroma. As someone who has experienced a childhood riddled with sexual abuse, I know—just as Rita must know—that there are far worse things than death. Spending the rest of her life in prison is one such thing.

Each week I checked the Illinois Department of Corrections Web site to see whether Rita was still alive. She told me, in the early fall of 2001, while we were sitting in the visit room—a place where secrets are shared—that if her name and photograph were gone, I would know that she had killed herself. The Web site catalogues all prisoners, their photos, the crime or crimes for which they are currently incarcerated, and any prior convictions. All changes are quickly recorded. It seems queer that I have it bookmarked under "favorite Web sites"; now it's my most feared.

The farmland that surrounds the Dwight Correctional Center retains the same winter landscape it did nearly fourteen years ago. Barren trees circle a farmhouse; winter wheat breaks through the snow; flat land stretches outward into a distant gray. Except for an occasional rabbit crossing the open field, the area appears lifeless. Just the other side of a tall chain-link fence topped with rows of barbed wire is where Rita lives in a six-by-nine-foot cell.

Unlike farmers dressed in long johns, bib overalls, a sweatshirt, and a Rice's Feed Store cap who circle tables at the local coffee shop and plan for the coming spring, Rita does not talk about crop rotation or which brand of seed corn can withstand a summer drought. She wonders only whether she will survive.

Aside from someone stepping forward and admitting guilt, Rita is left with little hope. The Illinois Supreme Court could reduce her life sentence, like they had done for Richard, to sixty years, leaving her eligible for parole in thirty years. Subtracting her fourteen years served, she would have sixteen to go. And then there is the possibility that the court might release her for time served. But what if that doesn't happen? What if she lives in a six-by-nine-foot cell for the rest of her life? Will she become what inmates call institutionalized, where hope disappears, where prison becomes your destiny, where you mutate into the shell of a cicada and your soul flies away? Or will she determine her fate? Will she choose to die?

She talked about this possibility before, while we sat in the visit room, circled by tables of inmates and visitors who talked, laughed, cried, and sometimes prayed with hands held tight. She knew the time and place and how life would pass. *It's all about hope,* I thought. *When hope is blocked and darkness crowds the sunrise, her day will end.*

Part Two: **Trial**

5   Bibles and Crossword Puzzles

May 1988. Rita was riding her midnight blue Yamaha 650 Special along a narrow, winding blacktop just a few miles west of her parents' house. White dogwood and purple redbud filtered through the woods, and the smell of freshly mowed grass filled the air. It was spring: a time of rebirth, of resurrection. And for Rita, it was a new beginning. One week earlier, Richard Nitz had been arrested for the murder of Michael Miley, and for the first time in years, she felt safe.

A gust of air pushed her way as a police car with flashing lights passed and stopped, forcing Rita to shut down her bike to avoid running into the ditch. A brown unmarked car was close behind. One man, dressed in a suit, stepped out of the unmarked car, and a duet of uniformed officers, one male and one female, crawled from the other.

"What's going on?" Rita said as she raised the bike and brushed herself off.

"We have a warrant for your arrest," answered the man in the suit.

"For what?" Rita asked.

"I don't know," the male uniformed officer said. "We were told to bring you to the Jackson County Jail."

Rita was led to the car, spread-eagled, and searched.

"Put your hands behind you," the officer demanded as he handcuffed Rita and then pushed her into the backseat. In front, a wire screen completed the cage that separated her from the two officers.

The car began to move. Rita remembered that several times, the driver accelerated, then hit his brake and accelerated again. Each time, she bounced between the back seat and the metal screen.

"What are you doing?" she yelled. "You're going to kill me."

"Shut up," shouted the officer as he continued the stopping and starting game.

Some thirty minutes later, they arrived at the Jackson County Jail, where Rita was pulled from the car and led to a room inside. She sat alone and thought, "They must want information about Richard. Why else would they bring me here?"

Minutes later, a woman dressed in a dark suit, looking more like a corporate executive than an officer with the Illinois State Police Special Investigations Unit, entered the room. She spoke softly. "Rita, you're not in any trouble. We just want to ask you about Richard. Can I get you some coffee?"

"Yes, that would be nice," Rita answered.

As Rita waited for her to return, a man she had not seen before entered the room. He walked to the table, turned, and stared. Only his tapping on the tabletop broke the silence. "Why are you looking at me?" Rita asked. "What do you want?"

"You're in a lot of trouble," he finally said.

"What do you mean?" Rita questioned. Her voice cracked while the detectives worked the good-cop, bad-cop routine. "The lady said that I wasn't in trouble and now you say that I am. I want to call my attorney."

"You don't need any attorney," the male officer shot back. "If you know what's good for you, you'll talk now."

Finally, the male officer stood, hurled a large law book toward Rita's table and left the room. "You'll get your damn attorney," he yelled.

Later that day, attorney Larry Beard arrived and, after meeting with the officer in charge, told Rita that she would have to spend the night in jail but not to worry. "You'll be released tomorrow," Beard promised.

At nine a.m., Rita, with eyelids swollen shut from a sleepless night, sat in the judge's chamber. "Rita Nitz," the judge said, "you are being arrested for the murder of Michael Miley and will be held on a $250,000 bond. If you're unable to post bond, you will be sent to the Williamson County Jail, where you will be held for arraignment."

Looking back, Rita said that she doesn't remember how she felt. "I guess it just didn't seem real. I was an alien in a strange world. My attorney told me that I would be out in no time and not to worry." Still, Rita admitted that she was afraid.

She was taken to the Williamson County Jail, where she was booked and fingerprinted. Next she was taken to the lower level, where she undressed, stood in the shower, and was deloused with a medicinal spray. She donned a loose-fitting brown jumpsuit and a pair of plastic shower shoes.

August 1971—another time, another place—and like most Sunday mornings in Palo Alto, California, the residents woke to the thud of newspapers landing on the front porch, cars traveling to nearby churches or the corner diner, and the sound of air brakes as an intercity bus came to a stop. But for some, it was different. Police cars, with lights flashing and sirens blaring, raced to the individual residences of twelve young men. A loud knock on the door was followed by the announcement that they were under arrest for violation of penal codes 211 and 459—armed robbery and burglary. Each was read his Miranda rights and led outside, where he was spread-eagled against the police car, searched, and handcuffed.

As part of a Stanford University study—later called the Stanford prison experiment—the Palo Alto police department had agreed to stage mock arrests of twelve male university students. Although the time of the arrests was unannounced, the students had previously agreed to participate in a two-week study in which twenty-four university students would play the roles of either guards or prisoners in a mock jail set up in the basement of the psychology building at Stanford University. By the flip of a coin, twelve students became prisoners and twelve became guards. The experiment, as described on the Web site www.prisonexp.org, was led by the Stanford psychology professor Philip Zimbardo and was intended to study the effects of incarceration on both the prisoners and guards: Why were some prisoners so disposed toward violence, and why were some prison guards so brutal?

The suspects were taken to the police station, where they were fingerprinted, booked, and placed in a holding cell. Next the prisoners were blindfolded and led to the mock jail, where they were stripped and forced to stand in the shower and undergo delousing. A nylon stocking covered their hair, giving the appearance of a freshly shaved head. Each was issued a loose-fitting jumpsuit and a pair of plastic shower shoes.

The Stanford prison experiment, planned to last two weeks, was stopped after six days. Professor Zimbardo wrote, "What we saw was frightening. It was no longer apparent to most of the subjects (or to us) where reality ended and their roles began. The majority had indeed become prisoners or guards, no longer able to clearly differentiate between role playing and self. . . . In less than a week the experience of imprisonment undid (temporarily) a lifetime of learning; human values were suspended, self-concepts were challenged and the ugliest . . . side of human nature surfaced. We were horrified because we saw some guards treat others as if they were despicable animals, taking pleasure in cruelty, while the prisoners became . . . dehumanized robots who thought only of escape, of their own individual survival and of their mounting hatred for the guards." The changes were swift and sweeping. How could the students, judged to be model citizens, revert to such primitive behavior? And if these changes occurred over six days, how did longer periods of incarceration affect Rita?

Rita was led to a cell block on the second floor at the north end of the Williamson County Jail. Each cell block was a rectangular area with a steel picnic table bolted to the floor. At the end of the table was a television set. Two five-by-seven-foot cells were on each side of the table. The cells had two metal bunk beds bolted to the wall and a stainless-steel toilet-and-sink combination bolted to the floor. The doors seemed to be constructed of heavy-gauge chicken wire and, except for lockdowns, were open from six a.m. to ten p.m., when prisoners were free to gather at the table and socialize. Still, Rita spent most of each day in her cell, reading the Bible and doing crossword puzzles.

For the next sixteen months, there were no windows. Night and day were dictated by the flip of a switch that controlled recessed fluorescent lights. I could only imagine Rita starting each day without a sunrise, missing the change of seasons and the feel of an evening breeze. Without sunlight, perhaps her fair skin faded to a chalk-white membrane with blue veins showing through, like lines on a road map.

Richard Nitz was held at the south end of the jail. Only a recreation room and two stripped cells used to contain potentially suicidal inmates separated the men and women. The guards provided the names of the prisoners to inmates of the opposite sex, and the men and women were allowed to exchange letters saying who they were, why they were being held, and whether they had any children. In a crude sort of way, they were a community.

When the men were in the recreation room, the women could hear their voices through the walls. Since Richard and Rita Nitz were not allowed to communicate, Rita was sent to segregation each time Richard was sent to the recreation room. She spent parts of three or four days a week in segregation, isolated from human contact, until Richard was transferred to the Menard prison some six months later.

Rita's attorney kept saying that it would soon be over and she would walk away. But she despaired. Rita worried about her son; she thought she would die. Finally she collapsed. Rita was told she was hypoglycemic and was issued a prescription for Tranzene. The medication supposedly would control her blood sugar levels. Not until some eighteen months later, when she underwent health screening at the Dwight Correctional Center, did Rita learn that Tranzene was an antidepressant.

"Looking back, most of the prisoners were medicated," said Linda Honeycutt, a former inmate incarcerated with Rita in the Williamson County Jail. Honeycutt stated in an affidavit I found in the court files that she witnessed other inmates taking medication three or four times daily. "I observed that after taking the pills given them, they lacked the ability to carry on conversation, think, or function in a normal manner."

Three or four months passed. Rita was taken to the recreation room to meet with an employee of Illinois' Department of Children and Family Services (DCFS). At the time, Rita's son, Chucky, was staying with her mother, Wanda Brookmyer. The man from DCFS sat across the table from Rita. "We're taking your son," he told her without explanation.

A jolt, like a jackhammer to the chest, woke Rita. "Richard," she yelled. Her screams swept through the jail. "I want Richard now. He's going to tell the truth that I had nothing to do with Michael Miley." Startled, the man from DCFS stood and backed away. "You're not going anywhere until this is settled," Rita insisted.

Guards quickly surrounded Rita. Two held her feet, two held her arms, another grabbed her waist. They carried her from the recreation room down the hall to the stripped cell and threw her to the floor. She remembered the angry guards and her screams, which must have filtered through the block wall that held back the male prisoners.

"Leave her alone," yelled one.

"Keep your fucking hands off her," shouted another.

They yelled, kicked, and threw anything that made a noise. Fearing a riot, the guards backed off and closed the cell door, leaving Rita on the concrete floor. Sounds of support seeped through the wall. "It's okay, baby, they're gone," said one prisoner. "Hang in there," said another. The voices continued. "You'll be okay. We love you, honey." Rita's wails shrank to cries, then to sobs, and finally to silence accompanied by the relentless hum of a fluorescent light.

6   Robin in a Cage

On September 21, 1989, a jury of twelve citizens decided how Rita Brookmyer Nitz, a twenty-nine-year-old woman charged with the murder of Michael Miley, would spend the remaining years of her life. How fitting that justice was decided in Metropolis, Illinois, the home of Superman, a larger-than-life TV and comic-book hero. Like me, other children of the 1950s learned that justice always prevailed under the watchful eye of Superman. And when Rita was sentenced to life in prison without parole, most people believed that good had triumphed over evil.

But over the years, just as the legend of Superman has waned and Metropolis has changed from a comic-book city to a riverboat community and finally to a nearly forgotten small town on the Ohio River, some people wondered whether justice was served. I, too, questioned Rita's guilt. But to believe her meant that our legal system had failed, an idea that made me uneasy.

Rita's trial was a long time coming. She was arrested in May 1988, one week after Richard's incarceration. At the time, Charles Garnati, the district attorney, requested a single trial with two juries: one for Richard and one for Rita. Her attorney, Larry Beard, inexperienced and swayed by Richard's attorney, decided to use Richard's defense story, which seemed strange, since Rita claimed that she was not with Richard on the night of the murder. This decision, plus the fact that Beard had never argued a murder trial, spelled disaster. Scared, confused, and desperate, Rita dismissed him. Richard's trial continued while the court appointed Robert Drew to represent Rita at a separate trial on a later date.

Except for Southern Illinois University, which employed some five thousand people, the geographical area of the crime included small communities supported by coal miners and farmers who struggled to grow crops on land better suited for lakes, rabbits, and spotted quail. Any cultural shift moved slowly through southern Illinois, an area—part of the Bible Belt—where daily life was as unchanging as hand-me-downs. As such, the residents were unaccustomed to horrific deaths like that of Miley and to the existence of a gay community, which up to then had been hidden.

At every beauty parlor, coffee shop, and even the Dixie Truck Stop, where truckers refueled their giant rigs before traveling a string of interstate highways that cross the Midwest, the story of the crime was told and retold. Richard Nitz was as notorious as Charles Manson. For this reason, Rita's trial was moved to Massac County, forty miles south of Williamson County, where Richard Nitz had been tried. But the move down Interstate 24, with the same judge, the same prosecutor, the same local TV stations and newspapers, made little difference.

Rita's trial unfolded in a two-story brick courthouse surrounded on three sides by a string of independent stores that struggled to survive. As in most small towns, the citizens, while yearning for the past, migrated to Wal-Mart and its lower prices, where they unknowingly pushed the dagger into the heart of the town square. Just west of the courthouse was the county jail and a small red building with a sign that said "The Superman Museum."

For sixteen days, Rita, filled with an evening of prayer, made her morning walk from the jail to the courtroom. But at the end of the day, the familiar feeling of doom returned as she sat in that lonely cell. Although she had no criminal record, jail was familiar; she had spent almost a year and a half in the Williamson County Jail, living like a robin in a cage.

After the trial began, Rita spent her weekday evenings in the Massac County Jail, while on weekends she was transported back to Williamson County. Although she had been taking Tranzene for the previous year, she was not given the antidepressant when in Massac County but did receive it during weekends at Williamson County Jail. As a result, Rita experienced nausea and dizziness and could barely function, let alone participate in her defense. This situation, plus months of incarceration, gave way to confusion. Still it is amazing that Rita does not remember much of the trial. It is as though she had not been there.

Each day, Rita and her attorney, Robert Drew, sat at one long table; Charles Garnati, the prosecutor, sat at another; to their right sat the jury. Judge Donald Lowery presided at the front of the courtroom, elevated and surrounded by panels of stained walnut.

Robert Drew, whom Rita called "Six-Pack Drew" because of his numerous complaints about hangovers, stood about five feet ten inches and tipped the scales at more than 250 pounds. With a baggy suit and a propensity to sweat, Drew appeared slipshod and uncertain. Quite often, Drew remained seated when he questioned a witness, appearing as though he were just not up to the fight. In contrast, Garnati, dressed in a gray tailored suit—light enough to withstand the sultry days of September—stood straight. Medium-built, five feet nine inches or so, with premature gray hair, Garnati looked dignified. His appearance, plus his aggressive nature and the confidence earned from a guilty verdict in Richard's trial, made Garnati a strong opponent.

The State of Illinois versus Rita Brookmyer Nitz: the entire state was against her, Rita thought. Eleven million people, the entire population of Illinois. "I just tried to survive," Rita later said as she recalled her feelings at the trial. "I didn't know who I was—what I liked or disliked. I was convinced that I wasn't human, just some sort of alien or something on this crazy planet."

As I read from the trial transcript, I imagined the movements—the gestures, the shuffling of feet, the occasional cough—that accompanied each word. Perhaps Garnati rose from his chair, and with a manila folder in his hand, walked across the wooden floor to a podium that faced the jury. He compared the state's case to a giant jigsaw puzzle.

"You are going to see that we spent hundreds of hours and interviewed hundreds of witnesses in our attempt to bring to you every piece of that puzzle, but what you must understand from the very beginning is that in any murder investigation there will always, always be a few pieces of that puzzle that we will be unable to give to you." Only three people will ever know the entire truth, he explained: Richard Nitz, Rita Nitz, and of course, Michael Miley, the deceased.

"I am going to take you into a world that probably most of you never knew even existed in Williamson County and throughout Southern Illinois. . . . The world I am talking about is the world of the homosexual in Southern Illinois. First of all, Michael Miley, you will see, at the time of his death on April 6th, 1988, had been a practicing homosexual for about three years in Williamson County in Southern Illinois. You will see that Richard Nitz, who at that time was the husband of the Defendant Rita Nitz, the evidence will show, he was an obsessive homosexual hater."

Garnati continued by explaining how Richard and Rita had formed a group called the Trog Club. Richard was called Trog, and Rita was called Trogette. And the purpose of the Trog Club, according to Garnati, was to harass homosexual men.

"If Richard Nitz asked Rita to leave her child, she did it," Garnati said as he looked Rita's way. "If he asked her to jump, she jumped. If he asked her to help him commit a brutal murder, she did it." He looked back to the jury. "Rita was Richard's partner in marriage, and Rita was Richard's partner in harassing the homosexual community." Garnati wrapped Rita and Richard together so tightly that the jury could not see one without the other.

Rita and her attorney sat stone-faced as Garnati described the underground homosexual community in which Michael Miley socialized with other gay men. Two Hearts, a local bar, and the men's restroom in the basement of the Southern Illinois University library were spots frequented by homosexual men. And four parking lots—the "big parking lot," Vaseline Alley, Little Tahiti, and Big Tahiti, all along Crab Orchard Lake and within a two-mile radius of Richard and Rita Nitz's double-wide trailer—rounded out their meeting places.

Garnati described Betty Boyer, a friend of the Nitzes, who allegedly saw Richard and Rita and Michael Miley together at a trailer where Richard knocked Miley unconscious with the swing of a baseball bat. "Before she takes that witness stand I want you to understand a little bit about Betty Boyer," Garnati explained. "She is not an educated lady. I don't even think she has got her high school education yet. She has trouble with numbers. She has trouble estimating dates and things that happened a month ago. She has trouble estimating times, estimating distances. You are going to see that she is not an educated lady. But you will also see that she is telling you the truth to the best of her memory." Garnati returned to his chair most likely pleased with his presentation, one that was similar to his opening statement at Richard Nitz's trial.

Robert Drew moved to the lectern and spoke. Richard Nitz was an ex-convict and an evil man who probably killed Michael Miley. But Rita Brookmyer Nitz was not involved. From a restraining order to an eventual divorce, Rita did everything she could to distance herself from Richard. Still, despite her efforts, Richard never left her alone. On several occasions, Rita called the Williamson County sheriff's office to remove Richard from her property. Each time, Richard was gone or in the process of leaving when the sheriff arrived some thirty minutes later. "The evidence will show that Rita was sexually abused by Richard," Drew said. "She was mentally threatened and coerced numerous times by Richard Nitz. Rita was never free from Richard."

Drew continued. "Betty Boyer, the prosecutor's main witness, was psychologically raped. Records will show that she was interrogated for hours and hours on several days. They threatened her. They were going to put her in jail for the murder of Michael Miley. They were going to take her kids away from her. Finally, Betty Boyer broke. She came up with a story that was choreographed by the prosecution. She gave them the story they wanted."

Finished speaking, Robert Drew closed his folder and returned to his seat next to Rita. Members of the jury twisted in their chairs. "The opening statements are made by the attorneys to acquaint you with the facts they expect to prove during the trial," Judge Lowery said. "And any statement made which is not proven by the evidence should be discarded. The court will recess for fifteen minutes."

7 Apples and Oranges

Richard Miley, a retired civil engineer for the state of Illinois and Michael Miley's father, sat in the witness chair. Deep-set wrinkles cut into his face, particularly the corners of his eyes, showing the signs of stress and deep thought rather than the passing of time. Richard described his family: Steven, a forty-two-year-old son from his first marriage, and with his current wife, Peggy, Keith, age thirty-one, Marilyn, age twenty-nine, and Mark, age twenty-three—the twin brother of Michael Miley.

Richard Miley talked about the night of April 6, when he saw Michael for the last time. The five of them—Michael, Mark, Peggy, Richard, and Richard's mother—had dinner at their home around five thirty p.m. Michael, wearing a black and tan jacket and blue jeans and driving his 1972 Chevrolet four-door Impala, left the house at seven forty-five to attend an eight o'clock choir practice at the Elm Street Baptist Church.

When asked whether Michael owned a watch, Richard identified a gold Timex quartz wristwatch found in the console of the Plymouth Barracuda parked in the Nitz garage. "I bought that watch for myself, but it didn't suit my needs," he said. "So I sold it to Mark, and he later gave it to Michael. The three of us were always selling or trading or sharing something." He described Michael as slightly built at five feet eight inches and 120 pounds and as someone who was not a fighter but did not hesitate to speak his mind. At the time of Michael's death, Richard was unaware that Michael and Mark were homosexual, and he knew nothing of a homosexual community.

Like her husband, Peggy Jo Miley spoke affectionately of Michael. "He loved to sing," Peggy said. "Michael sang all through high school and the church choir for I don't know how many years. We both had choir practice that night. After practice, a couple of women stopped me. I was the church secretary, and they had things that they wanted to go into the church bulletin." Peggy hesitated, her head dropped. "I didn't see Michael leave."

Garnati showed Mark Miley a gold Timex quartz wristwatch. "The silver is rubbed off right where the clasp closes, and it fits my wrist exactly," Mark said. "There's no doubt. This is the watch that I gave to Michael."

Mark then identified a Sanyo AM-FM cassette player that he had installed when he owned the 1972 Chevrolet. The tension in Mark's voice lifted as he was asked about Michael's love for music. "Michael was always copying forty-five [rpm] records onto cassette tapes so he could listen to them in his car," Mark said. Garnati picked up a box filled with cassette tapes and carried them to the witness chair for Mark to see. "Yes, these were Michael's tapes," Mark said. He quickly recognized one marked "1979 Murphysboro High School Chorus Concert." As Mark thumbed through the box, he commented that *Manilow Magic* by Barry Manilow was one of Michael's favorites and that *Hooked on Christmas* was a collection of various artists. Mark identified tapes by Anne Murray, the Carpenters, and Judy Garland and one called *Bar Music of 1984*. He explained that he had asked Jimmy Reed, a disc jockey at Two Hearts, to copy some of the music played at the bar. "I made an extra copy for Michael. You can see my handwriting on the tape," Mark said. "Michael kept it in the glove compartment."

Mark and Michael, for the previous three years, had been part of the homosexual community in southern Illinois. Mark acknowledged the Two Hearts Bar at 213 East Main Street in Carbondale and the four parking lots around Crab Orchard Lake as places where they met other men.

"We had dinner at our parents' house," Mark answered, when Garnati asked him where he last saw Michael on April 6. He said that he had driven to Crab Orchard Lake earlier in the evening but did not see Michael at that time.

Robby Buttry, an employee at Allen's Hair Design in Marion, testified that on April 6 he saw Michael at Vaseline Alley, one of the parking lots at Crab Orchard Lake. Buttry, who had worked late that night, like many times before, drove to the lake to unwind. It was around nine p.m. when Buttry pulled into the lot, made a U-turn, and backed into a spot close to the water. A few feet to his right was another car, but the darkness prevented him from identifying the person sitting inside. Buttry lowered his window and heard the wind gently push water over the spillway. The longer he sat, the more his car filled with flying bugs. He turned on his dome light and saw the air peppered with buffalo gnats. "Buttry, is that you?" yelled the person in the adjoining car. "Yes. Edwin, is that you?" answered Buttry as he heard the familiar voice of his friend, Edwin Pierson.

The two of them talked back and forth, catching up on who was doing what and complaining about the taste of buffalo gnats. Minutes later, a Chevy Impala swung into the lot and parked no more than three feet from Robby's car. Moonlight filtered through the darkened clouds, allowing Buttry to recognize Michael Miley, whom he had met before. The three of them talked for fifteen minutes or so before they started their cars and drove away: first Michael, then Edwin, and finally, Robby. Both Robby and Edwin testified that they went home around ten p.m.

The prosecution wanted the jury to believe that Richard Nitz thought of the parking lots next to Crab Orchard Lake as his private domain. After all, he and Rita were married by the lake, their home was no more than a mile down the road, and the lake provided a site where Richard partied with his friends and reflected when he was alone. It was not a place he shared freely, certainly not with what Richard called "a bunch of faggots." But the homosexual community, in the 1980s and in this part of the Bible Belt, was limited to only a few spots where they could openly socialize.

Four parking lots rested between the western border of Crab Orchard Lake and Spillway Road. Eight-tenths of a mile south of Highway 13 was the large parking lot, an open area about the size of a football field with a boat ramp and picnic tables scattered about. And two miles south of Highway 13, just off Spillway Road, was a long, narrow gravel lane that cut through a woods and led into Vaseline Alley, a small, circular lot with a picnic table at one end and boat ramp at the other. Less than a mile farther down Spillway Road was Little Tahiti. Like Vaseline Alley, it was a small, circular lot at the end of a long winding lane two-tenths of a mile off Spillway Road, and as Roy Dulaney said, "it was spooky and dark even in daylight." During a full moon, when all shapes of shadows bent and twisted against an evening breeze, fear was as close as the water's edge. Little Tahiti, according to Dulaney, was the spot Richard checked on and cleared out at night, wanting to keep gay men away from the place where he had been married. "I heard a lot of crude verbal garbage fall out of Rick's mouth," Dulaney said. "And I saw him carrying a baseball bat late at night at that spot. But right after that night, I quit spending any time out there." Big Tahiti, five miles south of Highway 13, completed the set of parking lots used by the gay male community.

Mark Miley testified that he had seen Richard Nitz two times prior to Michael's death. One time was a summer night in 1986, nearly two years before the murder.

"There were five of us in a car," Mark said. "Mike Davis, Carl Tripp, a guy named Richard, myself, and there were one or two other people that I do not remember." They parked their car at Little Tahiti where, like many times before, they visited and waited to see other friends. There, standing at one end of the parking lot, was a group of four men and one woman. It was a clear night but not light enough that he could identify someone from a distance. Still, Mark said the people in the group appeared to be holding chains, baseball bats, and ice picks. "The man, who I later identified from police photos as Richard Nitz, walked up to the car window and asked us if we were fags."

"No, they're down at the other end of the parking lot," answered Mike Davis, the driver of the car. Nitz turned and walked back to his friends and asked the woman if that was one of them.

"I can't be sure," she said.

"Before Nitz could say another word, Mike started the car and we peeled out of the parking lot," Mark said.

Robert Drew asked Mark Miley whether the police had ever asked him to look at photographs of women to help identify the one he claimed to have seen at Tahiti. When Miley answered no, Drew rephrased his question.

"They didn't show you a picture of Betty Boyer or Earlene Young or Rita Nitz?" Drew asked.

"Not that I remember," Miley said.

Upon further questioning, Mark Miley admitted to Drew that he did not know whether the woman was Betty Boyer or Earlene Young, both friends of Richard's, or Rita Nitz. Nor could he tell if the woman was tall or short, was heavy or thin, had long hair or short hair, or wore a dress or jeans. He was only certain that it was a woman, a woman holding an ice pick.

When asked about Mark's story some thirteen years later, Rita said that she was not the woman that Mark Miley claimed to have seen. "Richard ran around with other women. And he had his own circle of friends that I didn't know. When we first got married, I wondered why he was gone so much. Later on, I just wanted him to leave." In a later conversation, Rita told me that she had been thinking about who the woman might have been. "Now that I think about it," she said, "I believe it was my brother, Charlie. He had hair that reached his shoulder, and from a distance, he could have been mistaken for a woman. And I remember that he took an ice pick from my mother's house. I imagine he used it to punch holes in tires. I think it was Charlie."

Garnati asked Mark Miley about another incident that took place at Crab Orchard Lake in 1987. Mark pulled into the big parking lot. Some friends, James McClure and Larry Weis, sat on the hood of their car, parked about two hundred yards west of Mark, and listened to their radio. Mark walked to a pickup truck next to the lake and talked with the driver, someone he had never met before. As they talked, Mark heard a commotion, turned, and looked in the direction of his friends. There, standing next to James McClure and Larry Weis, were Richard Nitz and two men, each carrying a baseball bat. As Richard smashed their radio, the truck pulled away and Mark ran to his car. When Mark began to drive away, Richard broke the windshield with a baseball bat; another guy hit the side mirror; the third man cracked the headlight.

Mark Miley's story mirrored charges of criminal damage to property, aggravated assault, and intimidation filed on May 29, 1987, by the state's attorney of Williamson County. As in Miley's account, James McClure, Lawrence Weis, and Mark Miley were named as victims of Richard's attack.

Charlie Brookmyer, Rita's nineteen-year-old brother, testified that Richard Nitz did not like gay men and called them "faggots." He talked about a time during the fall of 1986, when he and some of his friends drove to one of the parking lots where they saw Richard and Rita.

"Counting Richard and Rita, there were seven or eight of us," Charlie said. "We had all been partying and were pretty well loaded." Richard pointed out a group of four or five people across the parking lot whom he believed to be gay. Richard, Charlie, and two of his friends walked to the other group and ran them off. Charlie, while on the stand, admitted to carrying a weapon at the time. When asked whether Rita made any derogatory statements about gays, Charlie answered, "Not that I remember."

Betty Boyer said that in May 1987, Richard and Rita Nitz stopped by the trailer where Betty, her husband, and their three children lived. Richard asked Betty's husband, Charles Hooker, if he wanted to harass some homosexuals. Betty did not remember her husband's response but said that Richard, Rita, and Charles left later that evening and returned around midnight. Still, Betty didn't know where they had gone.

The local homosexual community had experienced harassment before, but the horrific nature of Miley's murder raised fear to a worried state. Some person or persons had attacked their community with a recklessness never seen before. Still, what happened on that spring evening, more than seventeen years ago, was a riddle. A man, whom I will call Martin McCormick, a member of the local homosexual community during the 1980s who knew Mark and Michael Miley, gave me a glimpse into the inner workings of his circle. He had frequented the Two Hearts Bar and the parking lots at Crab Orchard Lake and told me things I had never heard before. He said that the wrong brother might have been killed. McCormick's revelations were sudden, like thunder on a sun-filled day.

"I think poor Michael was in the wrong place at the wrong time," McCormick said. Michael Miley, according to McCormick, was a quiet, gentle man who lived in the shadow of others; Mark was an outspoken, abrasive man not afraid to make enemies. While Michael was drawn to seclusion, Mark sometimes performed as a female impersonator at the Two Hearts Bar.

"His performances were very suggestive," said McCormick. "This guy was over the edge."

McCormick's comments about Michael sided with those made by Paulette Curkin, who owned the Main Street East Bar—later known as the Two Hearts Bar—until November 1987. Curkin remembered Michael Miley as timid, as someone who came into the bar and stood behind people, hesitating to step forward. She often wondered how out of character it seemed for Michael to confront anyone, particularly Richard Nitz.

The two of us, McCormick and I, sat at a corner table in the Mélange coffee shop at seven p.m. on a work day. It was quiet. Two couples sat at tables across the room, and light jazz insulated our words from others. McCormick was friendly and open and shared some memories. During the 1980s, as McCormick explained, the homosexual community was pushed to the fringes of a society that believed in heaven and hell and thought some things should never change. It was an intolerant time that spawned secrecy. And too often, such concealment bred lies. A lovers' quarrel that ended with a black eye might produce a story of someone walking into a cabinet door; a smashed car window might be attributed to alleged harassment; and a murder might be blamed on thievery. Whether they were exclusively homosexual or were bisexual and stealing a few hours away from their wives, some men had things to hide. And this environment made the task of determining Miley's murderer all the more difficult.

For some gay men, Saturday nights, and sometimes Fridays, ended at the large parking lot next to Crab Orchard Lake. "Every Saturday," McCormick explained, "we put beer in our trunks and drove to the parking lot. We arrived around twelve thirty a.m. and left at two a.m." When asked about gay bashers, he seemed surprised. Except for the occasional yell from a passing car, McCormick said he never saw anyone with a baseball bat or experienced any threatening actions. "Oh, occasionally I heard of some confrontation at one of the smaller parking lots, but I didn't know if that was for real or if it was another example of a lovers' quarrel covered up." But in a later interview, after he had talked with friends, he told me that some of the community had been harassed at Little Tahiti—the smaller, more remote parking lot sometimes used for intimate meetings.

Like so many times before, interviews moved to theories about who killed Michael Miley. My meeting with McCormick was no different. I told him about the pathologist's puzzling report, describing how a sexual assault kit was used to determine that no sexual encounter occurred. Still, Miley's pants were unzipped and partially pulled down, and pieces of grass and crushed leaves were found in his pubic hair. Without hesitation, McCormick said that the report proved only that there was no oral or anal sex. It did not prove there was no sexual encounter. He went on to explain that it was commonplace for two men to undress and touch. "Maybe Michael sat on the ground with someone," he said. "That would not have been unusual."

"Would it have been like a heterosexual couple petting?" I asked.

"Yes, that's right," he answered. We agreed that Michael could have been the victim of a sexual encounter gone bad. It was another theory. McCormick added that Michael more than likely would have been with someone he knew.

I related a theory of J. R. Moore, a private investigator for the defense. Moore, while investigating the Miley murder, went to the Two Hearts Bar, hoping to find information about Richard Nitz. More than one person, according to Moore, told him that Richard came to the bar by himself, wanting sex with other men. Like Moore, Curkin heard the occasional rumor that Richard might have had sexual encounters with men. In response to the same question, Roy Dulaney said, "Rick was all over the map and you could not tell for sure what his orientation might be."

Garnati contended that the motive for Michael Miley's murder was Richard Nitz's hatred for homosexual men and that Rita was his partner in crime. During a conversation at the Dwight Correctional Center, Rita told me that her best friend, Roy Dulaney, was bisexual and that he felt confused and guilty about his sexual orientation. She assured him that he was perfectly normal and continued to lend her support. And then there was Dickie Daniels, Rita's gay uncle who had adopted his deceased sister's son. "We called Uncle Dickie's partner Auntie Don," Rita said as she smiled. Given her deep friendship with Roy and her fondness for Uncle Dickie, it is difficult to imagine her having any revulsion for the homosexual community.

But what about Richard? An investigative report taken when Richard was arrested for the murder of Michael Miley reported the following interrogation: "Have you ever hurt any homosexuals?" asked the detective.

"I slapped them around some, but I'd never hurt them," answered Richard. "That would mess up all my fun."

What if Miley's murder was all about hate? Although the Hate Crime Statistics Act of 1990 and the Hate Crime Prevention Act of 1999 were not passed until years after Miley's death, hate was as certain as a hot summer in southern Illinois. If not for hate, what would cause someone to commit such violence? Somewhere between dirty diapers and manhood, the killer had been filled with twisted thoughts. Maybe love was lost or turned inside out. In an interview with the Public Broadcasting Service printed at www.pbs.org, Karen Franklin, a forensic psychology fellow at the Washington Institute for Mental Illness Research and Training, sees a variety of reasons for hate crimes. People who share similar ideological views, thrill seekers, men looking to prove their manhood, and others who see homosexual people as predators can push the buttons of hatred.

Unlike the highly publicized 1998 murder of the young gay man Matthew Shepard, the Miley case did not receive national attention and for the most part remained within the boundaries of southern Illinois. Paulette Curkin, currently an advisor for the Saluki Rainbow Network, a local homosexual organization, said that Miley's murder did nothing to further the development of any federal or state legislation to protect the homosexual community. Three weeks after the murder, when Richard was arrested, people returned to their habits and life was the same as before.

"I don't think Richard hated homosexuals," said Mary Burns, an invented name for someone who knew Richard well. "In fact, he had a friend that was either gay or bisexual. To understand Richard, you must see people as apples or oranges." Burns went on to explain that when you peel an apple, you eventually come to the core. But when you peel an orange, you end up with nothing but pieces. "Richard was like an orange; he had no core."

Richard was in and out of prisons from 1971 to 1989, when he began serving his life sentence for killing Michael Miley. He served time in the oldest and toughest and scariest-looking prisons in Illinois: Joliet prison, built in 1858, and Menard prison, built in 1878. "If Richard had any core beliefs when he went in, they more than likely disappeared," Burns said.

During Richard's first stay at Menard, he joined a white supremacy group. "It didn't have anything to do with his beliefs," Burns said. "Membership meant protection and approval from other inmates." I imagined that Richard did or said whatever made his life more bearable.

I was later told by Wanda Brookmyer that Richard said he ran the gays away from the parking lots because of AIDS. "Richard said that mosquitoes could bite gays and later transfer the disease to members of his family. I didn't believe him," she said. "His first wife said that Richard was raped by some men when he was in prison. That sounds more likely."

"Each time that Richard was accused of harassing homosexuals," Rita said, "he was with his younger friends. He always sought their approval." Maybe Richard was just being Richard. Put him before a group, and the show began: Richard harassing homosexuals, walking through a black bar singing at the top of his voice "I'm Dreaming of a White Christmas," and raping his wife—all for the amusement of his friends.

8   Progress Cemetery

Each jurist sat still. The courtroom was quiet as each person strained to hear. Garnati moved closer to Richard Karber, one of the campers at Rocky Comfort. "Was there anything unusual about the dead body?"

"Yes, it didn't have a head on it," Karber said.

On Saturday, April 9, 1988, just three days after the murder of Michael Miley, a group of young people, ranging in age from nineteen to twenty-one or so, met at Rocky Comfort, a camping site just south of Crab Orchard Lake and between Devil's Kitchen and Little Grassy lakes. On this night, fifteen to twenty campers gathered to enjoy the outdoors, drink beer, and talk about what they would've, could've, and should've done if life gave them half a chance.

Rocky Comfort was an undeveloped area: good for hunting, fishing, riding dirt bikes, and camping but little more. The ground was laced with potholes and ruts from four-wheel-drive vehicles that plowed through during the rainy season, leaving the road barely passable. A small, unkempt graveyard called Progress Cemetery was at the south end of Rocky Comfort, and some five hundred yards north stood a weathered gray barn. On this night, sitting a hundred feet from Progress Cemetery, was what appeared to be an abandoned 1972 four-door, black-over-beige Chevrolet.

Earlier in the evening, the group set up camp at the barn. At midnight, when clouds passed through and the temperature dipped to the upper forties, ten to fifteen campers walked to the deserted car. Handheld flashlights and a full moon lit their way. "It was abandoned, and it looked like it had been burned, and the windows were smashed and the headlights were busted," testified Richard Karber. He explained that after they tried unsuccessfully to open the trunk, he used his Mossberg shotgun to fire four rounds of field load number eight shot into the trunk of the car. The trunk remained closed. Frustrated, the group rolled the car onto its top. Another camper pried the trunk lid open with an ax. A creaking sound was followed by the stirring of tall grass and a thud as a body fell from the trunk onto the ground.

After seeing the decapitated body, according to Karber, the campers returned to the barn, packed up their equipment, and went home, where Karber called the authorities and reported the incident. Maybe the passing of a year and a half since the incident or the fact that Karber already had testified in the trial of Richard Nitz explained his matter-of-fact account at Rita's trial. One can imagine each camper's reaction to such a sight: first the shock, like that of a startled hunter walking into a covey of quail, and then fear or absolute disgust.

Frank Cooper, a crime scene investigator, testified that he photographed the crime scene at Rocky Comfort and processed it for physical evidence. Cooper, an eleven-year employee of the Illinois State Police, estimated that he had processed between fifteen hundred and two thousand crime scenes. A middle-aged man, Cooper appeared at ease on the witness stand.

Cooper explained that he arrived at the edge of Rocky Comfort at 3:41 a.m. Because of the rut-filled road, he drove a four-wheel-drive pickup to the crime scene. Waiting at the overturned car was the Union County coroner, Darryl Rendleman; the Union County sheriff, Robin Dillon; Officer Stamp of the Union County Sheriff's Department; and special agents Sylvester and Nolen of the Illinois State Police. The burned-out car had no license plates or vehicle identification number, the windows were covered with soot on the interior, a partially burned jacket had melted into the kick panel of the driver's door, and the radio was missing from the dashboard.

"The body was a young white male, dressed in tennis shoes, blue jeans, maroon with white-striped underwear," Cooper said. "There was no shirt, no jewelry, and the head was missing."

At five fifteen a.m. on April 10, the car was transferred to Don's Auto Body in Anna, and the body was transferred to the morgue at St. Joseph's Hospital in Murphysboro, where Dr. Beverly Tsai performed an autopsy at one fifteen p.m. At the time, Cooper explained, the body had not been positively identified. But because of the relatively sparse population in the area and the fact that a missing person's report had been filed for a young man similar in stature to the body, officials suspected it was Miley's. After finger and palm prints of the body were obtained and compared with prints in the car and on a cologne bottle and a medication bottle obtained later in the afternoon from the Miley house, a positive identification was made. It was Michael Miley.

Cooper testified that a sexual assault kit was used to gather evidence during the autopsy. The kit contained oral and rectal swabs, hair standards, and any foreign debris that might have been on the body.

"Could you go through the kit and explain to the jury what is there?" Garnati asked.

"Yes," Cooper answered. "These two boxes contain the swabs that were used by Dr. Tsai. One being a swab of the larynx and one being a rectal swab. Dr. Tsai would make the swabs, and then I held the slides as Dr. Tsai would wipe the swabs on the slides, and then I sealed the slides myself. One being the larynx slide and one being the rectal slide."

"Please continue," Garnati said.

"This bag contains a paper towel which contained debris from the pubic area," Cooper said. "You put a clean paper towel underneath the pubic area. These kits contain a brand new comb. You take the comb and comb the pubic area onto the clean paper towel, fold the towel up, package it, and submit it to the crime laboratory."

Rita, holding a yellow pad and pencil, made notes, searching for flawed testimony that might provide an opening, an opportunity, to cast doubt on the state's case. But at times, Rita's mind drifted like floating leaves in late fall. The on-and-off effects of antidepressants, sixteen months of incarceration, separation from her son, and an attorney who said to speak to no one wore her down.

The district attorney seemed to move in slow motion, pulling words and thoughts from each witness like warm taffy. The jury sat stone-faced, turning their heads from Garnati to the witness, then back to Garnati, and then to the witness again. Rita awoke from her clouded thoughts, only to wonder what she had missed.

Later, when questioned by Robert Drew about the clothing found on Michael Miley, Cooper explained, "The pants were slightly down on the hips and open, the fly was open and the button at the top of the Levi pants was undone."

"You testified earlier about pubic debris that was collected on a paper towel," Drew said.

"There was hair and what appeared to be some dirt fragments or some type of plant material," Cooper answered.

"In the years of your experience and your education and so forth, is it at all unusual to find dirt and plant material and debris in the pubic area of a person deceased?" Drew asked.

"You don't find that as a general situation," Cooper answered.

Garnati objected when Drew asked whether this suggested that the deceased might have met his demise at a time when he was unclothed or partially clothed or had his pants down. The judge sustained his objection.

Beverly Tsai, a pathologist employed by Southern Illinois Medical in Belleville, followed Cooper to the witness stand. With years of medical experience that included more than six hundred autopsies, Dr. Tsai was considered an expert in the field of pathology. A petite, dark-skinned woman dressed in a navy-blue suit with her black hair pulled into a bun, she was asked whether there were any injuries or wounds besides the missing head. "The body showed some blood on the neck area and also dried blood that drained out on the torso," she said. "There was some degree of discoloration, which was caused by decomposition on the abdominal wall." Tsai added that the lungs were a pinkish color, not the normal red. "After given a history that the body was put in a trunk of a burnt car, I had a feeling that there was some combination of hemoglobin with chemical or carbon monoxide type substance. A pinkish red or cherry red color makes us start to suspect there was carbon monoxide intoxication." Since there was not a large amount of blood found on or near the body and there was no evidence of a struggle, Tsai believed that Miley was dead before the head was cut off. She also testified that there was no evidence of sexual activity and that, finally, the cause of death could not be determined because the head was missing.

Rita later wondered why Drew never asked how a body allegedly struck five or six times with the downward blows of a baseball bat would not have marks on the shoulders. During Richard's trial, Betty Boyer had testified that Miley, after falling to the ground, was struck another ten to twenty times with the baseball bat.

During Richard's trial, Larry Broeking, Richard's attorney, asked Dr. Tsai whether there were any wounds, bruises, or scrapes on the body, and whether there was evidence of broken fingernails, which might indicate a struggle by Miley to escape from the trunk of the car. He asked Tsai whether she could say with a reasonable degree of medical certainty that Michael Miley died from a blow to the head. To each of Broeking's questions, Tsai answered no.

9   Cops, Cigarettes, and Black Coffee

It was April 27, 1988, just twenty-one days after the death of Michael Miley, when Judge Robert Howerton issued a search warrant for the residence of Richard and Rita Nitz, rural route 2, box 56, Carbondale, Illinois. Attached to the warrant was a photograph of the residence—the trailer, three vehicles, outbuildings, and a garage—that Phillip K. Sylvester, a sergeant with the Illinois State Police; ten police officers; and Frank Cooper, the crime scene technician, intended to search. The three vehicles included a 1974 beige Dodge Charger, a 1973 yellow AMC station wagon, and a gray AMC sedan with no license plate. The officers wanted to search the persons of Richard Nitz, Rita Nitz, and Betty Boyer, who had lived with the Nitzes during the previous month. Days earlier, Richard Nitz had been picked from a photo lineup as the man who used Michael Miley's credit cards to purchase merchandise at a Paducah, Kentucky, mall. The police suspected that Betty Boyer or Rita Nitz had accompanied him to the mall.

Early the next day, a group of cops—some smoking cigarettes and drinking black coffee—met at the Illinois State Police office in Marion,

Illinois, and plotted their strategy. Like a string of ants—single-file, centered, and resolved—their patrol cars crawled down Highway 13, weaved onto Spillway Road, and one mile down the road, turned right onto Pear Lane and stopped at the Nitz trailer. Officers, with guns strapped to their sides, crawled from the cars. Phillip Sylvester knocked on the door and placed a search warrant in Rita's hand. Only Rita and a small child were present.

The police were looking for merchandise purchased at the Paducah mall with Miley's credit cards and a set of Ace bandages allegedly worn by Richard Nitz on the evenings of April 7 and 8. Several items were removed from the trailer and later labeled as exhibits for the state.

> exhibit 56—set of Ace bandages found in cabinet in bathroom
> exhibit 57—USA Olympic, size 8½ shoe box found in the northeast bedroom
> exhibit 62—Reebok shoe box, size 6 M, woman's white and blue and gray, 4000 shoe, found in the northeast bedroom
> exhibit 64—a pair of Reebok tennis shoes, blue and white, were being worn by Rita
> exhibit 65—Skiva multicolored bikini found in the northeast bedroom (Upon cross-examination, Sergeant Sylvester said that although the swimsuit appeared similar to the one purchased with Miley's credit card, the Skiva swimsuit "did not appear to be extremely old or extremely new.")
> exhibit 66—blue Le Tigre underwear found in the northeast bedroom
> exhibit 67—black Le Tigre underwear found in the northeast bedroom
> exhibit 68—Levi Strauss denim jeans, waist 29, length 32, found in northeast bedroom
> exhibit 69—Levi Strauss denim jeans, waist 29, length 32, found in northeast bedroom
> exhibit 70—pair of Olympic USA, size 8½ tennis shoes found underneath kitchen table

Officers testified that Rita was cooperative and assisted by signing a consent-to-search form needed to examine a 1971 Plymouth Barracuda parked in their garage and not included in the original warrant. In the garage, the officers sifted through some fifty garbage bags filled with an assortment of things from trash to boxes and sales tags later matched to items purchased at the mall. Suspicious items were labeled and logged as exhibits for the state.

exhibit 33—Timex gold-colored watch found in the console of the Plymouth Barracuda parked in the garage
exhibit 34—ten cassette tapes
exhibit 46—Sanyo AM/FM cassette stereo
exhibit 47—knife found in toolbox in garage
exhibit 49—packaging materials, underwear boxes and various containers for cloth items of merchandise found in the garage

A wooden baseball bat was found in the Dodge Charger, and a shovel with a questionable stain was found leaning against the garage wall.

exhibit 48—stained shovel
exhibit 50—baseball bat

Days earlier, the police were told by an unidentified source that Richard and Rita Nitz had placed a hundred-dollar deposit on a trailer in Tilden, Illinois. When asked about the Tilden trailer, Rita acknowledged the deposit and, according to Sylvester, gave them the keys to the trailer and authorized a search. Rita later told me that she never intended to move to Tilden with Richard.

There was no furniture in the Tilden trailer, just a few pots and pans, cereal boxes, soda and beer cans, and ashtrays filled with cigarette butts. Standing along a living room wall was a stereo system with two Pioneer speakers, later confirmed as having been purchased with Miley's credit card.

Robert Burns, a deputy sheriff with the Jackson County Sheriff's Department, testified that he participated in the only search of the Nitz residence on April 28, 1988. Burns focused his search on the northeast bedroom. Some forty-five minutes later, Burns and Captain Carl Kirk, another officer in the search, moved to the kitchen, where Rita was sitting at an oval Formica table marked by cigarette burns along the edge. A cup and a full ashtray sat on the table, an overused coffeepot sat on the stove, and four metal chairs with red vinyl seats circled the table. A small girl sometimes sat in Rita's lap and sometimes played.

Burns told Rita that they were looking for items purchased with Miley's credit cards and asked whether she would talk with them. She agreed. Kirk read Rita her Miranda rights. The three of them were joined later by Sergeant Sylvester. I can only imagine Rita's thoughts as her home was searched, the three police officers sat at her table, others rummaged through her cars and garage, and a small child ran about.

Burns began the interview by asking whether Rita and Richard were together as a couple. According to Burns, Rita said that they had been separated since the end of January until about two weeks earlier. It was Burns's understanding that the separation had ended.

When asked whether she had a weapon, Rita said that she owned a pistol, which was in a box on top of the refrigerator. Burns testified at Rita's trial that when he went to retrieve the pistol, he found an empty gun box with the model name JenningsJ22 and the serial number 442207 printed on its side. But at the trial, no one could locate the box.

Hoping to apply pressure, Kirk told Rita that they would turn over all the items they found during the search to the Kentucky authorities. Burns said that Rita began to cry and insisted that at the time the cards were used in Paducah, she did not know they were stolen. Still crying, Rita said that a lot of people were involved in this incident and that she feared for her life. She asked whether she needed an attorney.

"You're not under arrest," answered Burns. "You don't need an attorney. We're just trying to find the truth."

According to Burns, Rita maintained that Danny Walker, a friend of Richard's, gave the cards to Richard for some work done on Walker's transmission and that she first saw the cards as they stuck out of a wallet on the coffee table in her living room. She told Burns that Glen Murphy, Danny Walker, Dickie Waide, Betty Boyer, Earlene Young, Richard Nitz, and the kids were in her trailer that night. And, as conveyed through Burns's testimony, Rita said that sometime after Michael Miley's body was discovered, Glen Murphy boasted that he had taken the credit cards from Miley before he hid the body in the woods and that Murphy did something to Miley to conceal his identity.

Burns said that on April 6 Murphy was working in Georgia or Florida, but Burns did not know whether Danny Walker or Dickie Waide had been asked to provide an alibi for the night of the murder.

Upon cross-examination, Drew asked Burns whether he had taped the interview with Rita. Burns answered no but said that he had taken notes. When asked what happened to the notes, Burns said they had been destroyed after he wrote his report.

"So we have to take your word on what was said during that interview?" asked Drew.

"Yes, that's right," answered Burns. "You have to take my word."

Throughout the rest of the trial, there was no mention, by either the defense or the prosecution, of Glen Murphy, Danny Walker, or Dickie Waide.

The differences between Rita's and Burns's recollections of the April 28 interview are significant. Throughout the trial, Rita contended that the gun had been in the box and that Burns took it with him. Burns said the gun was not there. And more important, Rita contends that she and Richard were separated and that she was afraid of Richard. Burns said that Richard and Rita were together.

In this instance, the jury was left to believe either Robert Burns, a seasoned law enforcement officer, or Rita Nitz, a woman whom the prosecutor had called Trogette and who was alleged to be the coleader of a vicious club. On the surface, the decision was easy. But after some fourteen months of studying this case, I found the answers unclear.

On April 4, 1988, two days before Miley's death, Deputy McDonald and Sergeant Hines reported a shooting attack at the second lake entrance south of the spillway. Frank E. Hilt, the victim, alleged that while he was parked in the parking lot, three white males in a silver two-door Ford pulled up beside his car and demanded that he open his door. When he refused, one suspect fired some type of weapon into his car. All three suspects were in their teens to early twenties. The shooting suspect had a slim build and long dark hair, and the driver was overweight, with a mustache and glasses.

On May 9, 1988, Hilt was interviewed by Detective Lawrence A. Eaton. Again, the victim described the suspects as being three white males in a single car. The story was the same.

One year later, when asked about the shooting incident, Robert Burns testified that two white suspects were in one car and that Richard and Rita Nitz were in a second car. Since this testimony was contrary to the two police reports, Burns either was mistaken or was trying to place Rita at the crime scene.

Drew never objected to Burns's statement that Rita was present at the April 4 shooting incident. And upon cross-examination, Drew never asked Burns why his story of two vehicles—one with two white males and the other with Richard and Rita—conflicted with two police reports. The jury was left with little choice but to believe that this incident was just another example of Rita having accompanied Richard when he harassed gay men.

Sandra Cole Neal, a sales clerk at the J. C. Penney store in the Paducah mall, identified a sales receipt she had issued to a man and woman on the evening of April 7, 1988. Neal remembered this particular sales slip because it was signed in the wrong place by a man whose hands were wrapped in Ace bandages.

"Because his hands were wrapped with bandages, I was not going to ask him to sign again," Neal said.

She remembered the man as being white, in his early thirties, of medium build, approximately five feet seven inches tall, and weighing about 150 pounds. About the woman she could remember only that she was white, was about the same height as the man, and had brownish-blond hair. Garnati showed Neal a set of Ace bandages that she identified as similar to those worn by the male.

According to Neal, the woman pulled a J. C. Penney credit card from the back pocket of the man's worn jeans. Neal matched sales receipts with tennis shoes, blue jeans, and men's and women's underwear found at the Nitz residence.

Elizabeth Mitchell, also a sales clerk at the J. C. Penney store, identified a sales receipt she had issued to a man and a woman on the evening of April 8, 1988. Like Sandra Cole Neal, she said the transaction was conducted by a man who appeared to be in his thirties, stood about five feet six inches, weighed about 150 pounds, and had shoulder-length black hair. His hands had been wrapped in Ace bandages. Mitchell identified Richard Nitz as the man who used Michael Miley's credit card but could not remember the woman whom Nitz called his wife. When asked how the couple was getting along, Mitchell answered, "Fine, laughing and talking." She matched a sales receipt with bikini underwear found at the Nitz residence.

Margo Fondau, a sales clerk at the Sears store in the Paducah mall, identified another sales receipt issued to a man and woman on the evening of April 8, 1988. Her description of the man was similar to those of the other two clerks—white male, midthirties, five feet seven, 150 pounds, shoulder-length hair that appeared dirty, and hands wrapped in Ace bandages. She later identified Richard Nitz from a photo lineup. Although Fondau could not recall the woman, she said the man referred to her as his wife. Fondau testified that the couple used Miley's credit card to purchase two Pioneer stereo speakers, bikini swimwear, and two pairs of jeans.

Eloise Staley, another sales clerk at Sears, identified a sales receipt issued to a man and woman on the evening of April 8, 1988. When asked whether the couple was unusual in any way, Staley answered, "The man looked like he had been in an accident. He had both hands bound." Staley, too, identified the man from a photo lineup as Richard Nitz but could not remember the woman. She said the unidentified woman took the credit card from Richard Nitz's billfold and handed it to him. The woman then returned the billfold to his shirt pocket and "gave it a tender pat." They purchased a pair of women's Reebok tennis shoes, size six, later found on Rita during the April 28 search.

10 "Sometimes she called me Sis"

On July 3, 1988, Betty Boyer wrote to Rita Nitz: "I really can't believe all this is happening. The police are still coming around and asking a bunch of questions about all of this shit that is going on. Sorry I haven't written before now or been to see you, but the only reason why I haven't come to see you is because I'm afraid that the police is going to think I had something to do with this also. Larry [Beard] has already told me that they are going to put the rap of this on me also...." The letter was introduced as evidence in *People of the State of Illinois v. Rita Nitz*. At the time, Rita did not know that on May 6, Boyer had implicated her in the murder of Michael Miley and that Boyer would be the state's star witness.

Even today, some sixteen years after the trial, Rita cannot understand why the jury believed Betty Boyer's testimony. And to look at the trial transcript, it is hard to envision a guilty verdict without Boyer's eyewitness account. The cause of death was unknown, leaving the murder weapon in doubt, and no forensic evidence was available. In his closing statement, Garnati acknowledged the importance of Boyer's testimony. "Either Betty Boyer is telling the truth or Rita Nitz is telling the truth," he said. "... There is no gray area. It is black and white. One of them is telling the truth, one of them is absolutely not telling you the truth. I submit to you that Betty Boyer, when you look at all the evidence in this case, is the one telling the truth."

In his opening statement, Garnati portrayed Boyer as uneducated, questionable in her memory, and unsure of figures and measurements. But in spite of everything, she told the truth. Drew, puzzled by how anyone could believe Boyer's story, assailed her credibility.

Rita, with Robert Drew at her side, sat behind a wooden table while Betty Boyer, wearing a dress and shoes borrowed one year earlier from Rita, sat in the witness chair. According to Wanda Brookmyer, the state's star witness was wearing Rita's clothes. Behind Rita were her parents, Wanda and Galen Brookmyer. And at their side was the Reverend McCool, a regular visitor of Rita's at the Williamson County Jail and one who never doubted her innocence. Boyer told the court that she was unemployed, was working on her GED, was married to Charles Hooker, and had three children: Rose Marie Hooker, age six; Linda Sue Hooker, age five; and Charles Joseph Hooker, age three. She recalled meeting Richard, Rita, and Rita's twelve-year-old son, Michael Charles Hayward, on May 27, 1987, because it was the day Betty and her husband reunited after a separation and were living at the Lakewood Trailer Park on Apple Lane, right off Spillway Road.

In early January 1988, after Betty had left her husband again and temporarily sought shelter at the local women's center, Richard and Rita let Betty and her three children move into their four-bedroom trailer on Pear Lane. Weeks later, when it became obvious that Richard and Rita were having marital problems, Richard moved out and Rita filed for a divorce. Rita obtained a restraining order against Richard and asked her friend, Roy Dulaney, and her cousin, Larry Brookmyer, to stay with her for protection: Dulaney at night and Brookmyer during the day. While Betty and her three children lived with Rita, Dulaney became attached to Betty's children and a romantic relationship developed between him and Betty. "I don't know how romantic it was," Rita later told me, "but they were sleeping together."

When Betty shifted her attention to another man, Dulaney moved out. "I couldn't take it anymore," he said. "It hurt too much."

Rita believed that Betty was seeing Richard. During one of my visits to the Dwight Correctional Center, Rita said people called Betty "a buck-ninety-five."

"What do you mean?" I asked.

"Betty could be had for a $1.95."

Rita purchased a gun for her protection, a gun that the state later claimed was used to kill Michael Miley. She told me that Dulaney went with her on March 24, 1988, to the Shooter's Pro Shop, a firearms business in Carbondale, where she bought a twenty-two-caliber handgun. Dulaney later claimed that he did not remember going with Rita on that day but that he often accompanied her when they went to pawnshops, gun stores, or anyplace else just to pass the time. He kept a journal, recording each day's activities and thoughts, and said it would show what he was doing on that day.

A year passed before I heard from Dulaney again. He told me that he had received pressure from family members to ignore my calls. Although Dulaney found his journals that covered the early months of 1988, he could not account for March 24. When Dulaney and Betty broke up, he became depressed and made no entries in his journal from March 20, 1988, to April 5, 1988. Still, Dulaney was certain that he did not go with Rita to buy a handgun.

At Rita's trial, an employee at Shooter's Pro Shop, Robert Brian, testified that he sold Rita a handgun on March 24, 1988, but could not remember the man who accompanied her. And Curt Ehlers, a deputy sheriff with Jackson County, testified that he was in the Shooter's Pro Shop on March 24 and remembers Richard Nitz coming in with an unidentified woman. The state believed the woman was Rita. Rita still maintains that she was with Dulaney.

In the courtroom, Garnati asked Boyer whether she ever went to court with Rita. "I went to court with her when Richard had raped her," Boyer answered. She claimed to have seen Richard hit and rape Rita and throw her against the trailer.

"After Rita filed for divorce," Garnati asked, "did you ever talk to Rita about her marital problems?"

"I told her that she would be better off if Richard was not around her, the way he was abusing her, and that she would not be in so much trouble if she was not with him." But when asked whether Rita followed her advice, she answered, "Somewhat."

Betty testified that Richard was calling Rita in mid-March 1988. "At times Rita would be scared and she would cry," Betty said. "But Rita would still go ahead and meet him for coffee because he wanted to talk to her." When Betty believed that Richard and Rita might get back together, Betty moved in with Earlene Young, a woman who shared her history of abuse from men and who lived in a trailer on Cherry Lane next to Spillway Road. Since Betty kept most of her clothes at Rita's, she made frequent trips across the three lawns and gravel driveway that separated the trailers. When asked whether Richard had moved in with Rita, Betty said she did not know but on occasion saw a pair of pants and a shirt that Richard wore when he spent the night. Thirteen years later, Rita said that Betty never moved out of the trailer and that all of Betty's stuff was kept in her trailer or in the garage. Still, Betty was gone a lot in the evenings and Rita never knew where.

Garnati asked Betty to explain what she was doing on April 6, 1988, the day of Miley's death. At twelve thirty p.m., according to Betty, she went to the Jackson County Courthouse for a traffic fine. Since she did not own a car, Earlene offered to take her. But when Earlene's car failed to start, they borrowed Richard's. They returned to Rita's house between three and three thirty p.m.

"Only Rita and her son, Chuckie, were there," Betty said. "Chuckie was sick and had stayed home from school. She asked me if I would babysit later that evening." Betty went to Earlene's trailer, changed clothes, ate some food, and returned to Rita's around six p.m. Rita, Richard, and Chuckie were there. "I sat down and had a cup of coffee," Betty said. "Rita and I talked for a few minutes." At six thirty Rita and Richard left in their Plymouth Barracuda, drove to John Barwick's car lot in Carterville, and returned some thirty minutes later.

"They came back and Rita came inside the trailer," Betty said. "Rita walked into the kitchen and got a gun off of the top of the icebox and went back out. Rita returned to the car and handed the gun to Richard." Betty said that Richard and Rita drove away and returned between nine thirty and ten p.m. "I'm certain about the time. I gave Chuckie his medication a little after nine p.m. and they returned about ten or fifteen minutes later."

Betty recalled hearing loud music, walking onto the front porch, and seeing Richard and Rita drive up in their Plymouth Barracuda. The Barracuda was parked about five feet behind their Dodge Charger. Rita got out of the Barracuda and went directly into the trailer to use the bathroom. Richard was still outside when another car pulled into the driveway, backed out, and parked on Pear Lane. Still on the front porch, Betty watched as a man left the third car and stood in the driveway. Richard went to the Dodge Charger and removed a wooden baseball bat from the back floorboard. At that point, Betty, saying to herself that it was none of her business, turned around and went inside the trailer.

"What were the lighting conditions that night out in the driveway?" Garnati asked.

"The porch light was on and they had a security light," Boyer answered.

Earlier, a local weather operations manager testified that at 8:54 p.m. on April 6, 1988, northwest winds were blowing at seventeen miles per hour with gusts from twenty-three to twenty-four. Large tree limbs were rustling, and small waves and crests were forming on nearby lakes. The sky was overcast.

"Now when you went back into the house, where did you go?" Garnati asked.

"I walked over to the window to see what was going on," Boyer said.

"Okay, did you hear anything being said out there at about that time?" Garnati asked.

"Yes," Boyer said. "I heard Richard holler out at the man to get his fucking ass off of his property; that he wasn't nothing but a faggot, and if he didn't he was going to kill him."

During Richard Nitz's trial, a former neighbor of Nitz's, Robert Baumbeck, testified that his home sits about one hundred feet from the Nitz trailer. He recalled being home April 6, 1988, and said that he went to bed between nine thirty and ten p.m. There was nothing unusual to make him think something had happened; there were no voices or gunshots or screams. Baumbeck did not testify at Rita's trial.

Boyer said that Richard hit the other man several times across the back of the head with a baseball bat. And when the man fell on the concrete slab next to the steps, blood poured from his head.

"What was Rita doing?" Garnati asked.

"She wasn't doing anything but standing there being quiet," Boyer answered.

"Did you go out and try to help the man?" Garnati asked.

"No. I was scared," Boyer said. "I thought he might hit me with the baseball bat." Boyer described standing at the window and watching Richard walk to the man's car, remove the keys, and open the trunk. After telling Rita to pick up the legs, Richard and Rita loaded the body into the trunk of the young man's car. Richard got into his Barracuda, and Rita got into the man's car. After Richard backed out, Rita followed him down Pear Lane.

"What did you do next?" Garnati asked.

"I went back and sat down and turned the stereo on and I listened to the music," Boyer said.

"Did you call the police?" Garnati asked.

"No," Boyer answered. "I was scared."

Betty testified that she received a collect call from Richard Nitz around one a.m. He told her that his car would not start, and he wanted her to go ask Earlene to pick them up somewhere around Crab Orchard Lake. Betty said that she walked to Earlene's, gave her the message, and returned to Rita's trailer to stay with Chuckie.

But later testimony by John Johnson told a different story. Johnson, who lived five miles southeast of the Crab Orchard Lake spillway, testified that a man and woman knocked on his door at one a.m. in April 1988. The couple's car had broken down, and the man asked to make a collect call. Although Johnson could not remember the exact date, his telephone bill showed a call to the Nitz residence was made at 12:29 a.m. on April 8, more than a day after the incident.

Upon cross-examination, Drew asked Johnson whether police officers suggested the date was April 7. "They asked," Johnson said. "Yes, I think Captain Kirk asked if it could have been the 6th or 7th. I said that I don't know. Honestly, I don't know." Drew continued by asking Johnson whether the route from the Paducah mall to the spillway would go by his house. "Yes," Johnson answered. "That's the best route." It was clear that the telephone call was made when Richard and Rita were returning from the Paducah mall on April 8.

According to Boyer, Richard and Rita returned to their trailer at five a.m. on April 7. Rita went directly to bed, and Richard filled a bucket with hot soapy water and washed blood from the concrete slab. Betty said that she did not see Richard do anything with the baseball bat. She went to Earlene's trailer around six a.m. and woke Earlene so she could get the kids ready for school. Betty went to bed.

"Did you have any more contact with the Nitzes?" Garnati asked.

"Yes," Betty answered. "They invited me over for dinner and coffee."

"And why did you go back over there after seeing something like this?" Garnati asked.

"Because I did not want them to think that I had seen what they had done," Betty answered.

Betty said that the police began questioning her two or three days after the incident. On five or six different days, Betty was taken in for questioning and kept for several hours. She recalled the night at the Southern Illinois University police station when she was questioned by officers Curt Graff, Larry Eaton, and Monica Joast.

"It was May 6, 1988," Betty said. "I had been there for four to five hours."

"Now to be perfectly honest," Garnati said, "were any of those police officers rude to you that night?"

"Yes," Betty said. "Curt Graff kept telling me I was nothing but a lying bitch, and he had upset me, and I threw my cigarette case at him."

"Now after that happened," Garnati said, "where did you go?"

"Monica took me downstairs to try to calm me down and let me use the restroom," Betty said.

After the officers told Betty that Richard had been arrested, she told the police about the incident at the Nitzes' trailer. Five days later, Rita was arrested.

Drew made numerous comparisons among Betty Boyer's testimony at Richard's trial, her testimony at Rita's trial, and her recorded interview with Ron Roach, a special investigator for the Richard Nitz defense. The inconsistencies were numerous. Betty testified at Rita's trial that the incident at the trailer, when Richard allegedly hit Miley with the baseball bat, lasted ten minutes. But at Richard's trial, she said it took some thirty to forty-five minutes. Betty testified that Chuckie was sick and had not attended school on April 6. But at Richard's trial, she said Chuckie rode the school bus home around four p.m. on that day. Betty testified that after Rita filed for divorce, Richard did not come by the trailer. But at Richard's trial, she said he came to the trailer, causing Rita to call the police on numerous occasions. The inconsistencies continued when Betty testified that at six thirty p.m. on April 6, Richard and Rita left to take care of some personal business; at Rita's trial, they went to John Barwick's car lot; and when talking to Ron Roach, they went to J.T.'s to work on a motorcycle. In addition, Betty's time line for the evening of April 6, 1988, changed from one trial to the other.

Drew placed into evidence two letters Betty had written to Rita during early July 1988, when Rita was in the Williamson County Jail. In the letters, Betty referred to her poor vision and her need for eyeglasses.

"For the record," Drew said, "do you have corrective lenses on your eyes?"

"Yes, sir, I do," Boyer answered.

"Okay, when did you get those glasses?" Drew asked.

"I got them in May of 1988," Boyer said.

"That would have been after this incident?" Drew asked.

"Yes, sir," Boyer said.

"Were your eyes in bad shape on April the sixth?" Drew asked.

"No, they was not," Boyer said.

"Did they just go bad on you overnight?" Drew asked.

"No," Boyer answered. "I've been having problems with my eyes for the past few years because I was working with chemicals a lot when I was working for a plant and they told me I had an eye physical to be done and that's when they noticed I had to wear glasses."

"When did they say you needed glasses?" Drew asked.

"About two or three years ago," Boyer replied.

"You needed glasses on April 6 of 1988, is that correct?" Drew asked.

"Yes, but I could not get them until I was able to go to my eye doctor appointment," Boyer said.

"How did your eyes bother you?" Drew asked.

"Everything looked blurry to me," Boyer said. "And they start burning and itching, and they just told me I have to wear glasses."

"Did you have more problems at night or during the day or was there any distinction?" Drew asked.

"Both eyes were having problems during the day and night," Boyer replied.

"Is that part of the reason you were unable to identify the person you saw that night?" Drew asked.

"No," Boyer answered. "The person was more or less in the dark."

Drew asked Boyer if she let her children stay with Rita after the incident at the Nitz trailer, and she said that her younger daughter, Linda, had spent overnights with Rita. "You weren't worried about your children being in the same household with a person you described as a murderess?" Drew asked.

"No, I was not," Betty answered. "Rita thought very much of my children."

When asked about her social life around April 6, Boyer said she had been dating Ronnie Eugene Skelton. Upon further questioning, she acknowledged that on April 7, no more than twenty hours after the alleged beating of Michael Miley, she went on a date with Ralph Kraft. Boyer bristled and shot back, "What do my boyfriends got to do with the murder?" The prosecution objected, and the judge sustained the objection.

Boyer said that while Rita sometimes met Richard at public places, she tried to keep him away from the trailer. Betty told of an incident when Richard, who had been drinking heavily, stopped by Rita's trailer with a baseball bat and threatened to smash everything.

When questioned by Garnati, Boyer admitted that in July 1988, one month before testifying at the Richard Nitz trial, she was jailed overnight for a charge of simple battery. She told the jury that a twelve-year-old boy was riding his bike up and down Cherry Lane, the road in front of Earlene Young's trailer where Betty and her kids were staying. "I pushed the kid down because he was verbally calling my oldest daughter names," Boyer said. Upon cross-examination, Drew asked Betty why she was turned loose the next morning. "They told me to get my stuff together, that I was free to go and the charges was dropped." When asked if she had been arrested before, Boyer said that she had been arrested several times for traffic fines and contempt of court.

Drew asked Boyer whether she had been threatened by the police during questioning about the death of Michael Miley. "Curt Graff is the one that threatened me," Boyer answered. "He told me that if I did not start telling the truth, because he knew that I knew something about it, that he was going to call DCFS and they would come get my kids and throw me in jail and lock me up, and that I would never get out." Boyer also said that she had been interviewed by the police on six or seven occasions, each session lasting two to six hours.

Drew led Betty Boyer through the evening of April 6. With some imagination, the jury saw Boyer standing at the window inside the trailer, straining to see through the moonless night illuminated by a hundred-watt porch light and a security light mounted on a pole several feet away. Boyer described Richard Nitz, wielding a baseball bat with both hands, swinging in a downward motion as he administered five or six blows to the back of Miley's head.

"At the time that all of these baseball licks were being hit with both hands, you were in this window?" Drew asked.

"Yes," Boyer replied.

"Okay, and he was about here by the stairs?" Drew asked as he pointed to a visual aid.

"Yes," Boyer said.

"Were you able to make any observations about any change in his appearance?" Drew asked.

"No, I was not," Boyer said.

"Did his head appear to be in the same shape as it was before this baseball bat business started?" Drew asked.

"No," Boyer said.

"What was different about it?" Drew asked.

"I don't remember," Boyer said.

"Would it have been crushed or caved in?" Drew asked.

"It was caved in," Boyer said.

Betty Boyer's letters written to Rita in July 1988 were interesting not only for Boyer's remarks concerning her vision but also for her emotional detachment. She told Rita that if she saw Richard, to tell him she said hi. And this was after Boyer allegedly saw Richard beat Miley almost to his death. At the time of the letters, Rita was unaware that Boyer had implicated her in the death of Michael Miley and that Boyer would be the state's star witness.

> July 3, 1988
>
> Dear Rita,
>
> Hi, how are you doing. Fine I hope. I really can't believe all this is happening. The police are still coming around and asking a bunch of questions about all of this shit that is going on. Sorry I haven't written before now or been to see you, but the only reason why I haven't come to see you is because I'm afraid that the police is going to think I had something to do with this also. Larry has already told me that they are going to put the rap of this on me also.
>
> Well, anyway the kids are all doing fine. C.J. is almost potty broke. Linda and Marie are the same, fighting as usual. We are out here with a car that is broke down. The starter went out on it plus the valves went bad. About this money I owe you, I was cancelled out in June on my AFDC just been reinstated. As soon as I start receiving my checks like I'm supposed to if you will agree to it that maybe I could pay twenty-five dollars a month. I will because I heard . . . I will probably be seeing you sometime in August because I heard that's when the trial is going to be. But when you see me I will look different because I am wearing glasses now. Have to wear them all the time.

Well, I finally got DCFS off my ass. I told them to close my case and leave me the hell alone. Larry has typed up a letter to Springfield. Possibly for a hearing. The Bloemers are trying to do everything on Marie, saying that had never babysat for me while I was going to school. I seen them a couple of weekends ago and me and Lila got into it again. They had another warrant for my arrest out again. Now they are telling me I have got a ninety-three dollar fine to be paid by August 31st, plus I've also got a hundred and twenty-six dollar fine to pay. Hopefully you will understand why I haven't paid you yet, but I do intend on paying you.

Well, I guess you know in about two days I will be twenty-five years old. Well, I'm still seeing Ron. He is supposed to throw me a party, but I don't know for sure.

He is going to be getting a divorce from his wife. Guess Lisa is getting married August 24 or 25, and she also thinks she might be pregnant. I guess I better close for now. Hopefully you will be able to write me back at least so that I will know how you are doing.

Your friend always.

Betty.

I was unable to locate Rita's letter to Betty, which was probably destroyed or misplaced, as most letters are, shortly after Betty read it. Rita and I never talked about her letter and what it contained. Only six days after Betty's July 3 letter, Betty sent her second.

July 9, 1988

Dear Sis, Rita.

Hi, it's me again. Glad I heard from you. I was really surprised to hear from you. Didn't know if you was going to be able to write me or not. As for me coming up to see you, might be a bit of a problem cause right now the car is broke down, has been for two weeks now. I don't know how I would get up there unless you talked to Larry to see if maybe I could come with him sometime to see you.

Yes, I really do look different in glasses. I don't think I look that good in glasses but everybody else does. But I have to wear them all the time. They are blue framed. They are the same prescription that Earlene's is.

As far as the fines, they told me that they were traffic fines. The ninety-three dollars has to be paid by August 31. So far the judge doesn't know about the one hundred and twenty-six dollars, but I am going to pay it in September. You know I always try to stay out of trouble.

I wasn't much fun on my birthday. I was severely sick. No I did not get drunk as I had planned. Don't worry about the slug bugs, I have been getting Earlene on them left and right.

Well Richard Young, Earlene's son, has been with his dad since about the 26th of June. He's supposed to be back the 12 or 13 of this month. Jo Ann is supposed to be coming down here cause her son is there in jail for DUI. Heard that he was trying to commit suicide. Earlene can't wait until he comes home cause she misses him. Oh, Earlene told me to tell you she has almost put two hundred dollars worth of work on the car. She also says hi, and sorry to hear what has happened.

Linda says she wants to come home and Marie wants to see you, and C.J. he's just being a big pain. He's fighting with his sisters right now.

Well, I guess I finally got Chuck out of my life. He's no longer in Granite City because I sent him four letters and the last one I sent him got sent back. Nobody knows where he is at. But I turned him into the Social Security office. They are going to make me the payee of the check he gets for the kids.

Oh, yeah, Earlene also said that she wouldn't be able to make the car payment this month in order to get the car running and she hasn't had the title transferred yet, and she hopes everything works out for you. Oh guess what? Earlene told me Ralph David came by to see me yesterday (7-8-88) but I wasn't there but she said he had a motorcycle now. I missed him cause I went with Ron to get his truck licensed up.

Well I guess I had better tell you this also. I have quit drinking and smoking pot because I have a bleeding ulcer. I'm back on the tagoments like crazy. Probably will be all my life now.

Well I guess Chuckie is with his dad now. I bet that's a real bummer for you. I seen an article in the paper about Rick where they are calling him the alleged triggerman. I guess you ought to know this also so you won't think somebody stole it, but I've got your big trunk that was in the shed to store the kids and my winter clothes in. I really didn't think you would mind since we are so close, but don't worry I won't let anything happen to it. You know that I hope. Well, I guess I better close for now before I end up writing a book. Maybe this one is long enough for you.

Love always

Your sister, Betty

P.S. If you see Rick tell him we all said hi and to behave himself in there. Write back soon. Talk to Larry maybe I could come up with him to see you. Take care of yourself in there cause you mean a lot to me. Oh, what about the money I owe you? Will you agree to let me pay you twenty-five dollars until you're paid off?

"Sometimes she called me Sis," Rita said as we sat in the visit room at the Dwight Correctional Center. It was an early Monday in February 2001, before most visitors had arrived and before the smell of buttered popcorn filled the air. The sound of metal hitting metal resonated when doors slammed shut, and a prisoner drifted about the room, wiping each table with cleaner and paper towels. Our conversation had moved to Betty Boyer, Rita's best friend during the year before Michael Miley's death.

"We did things that sisters do," Rita said. A smile spread across her face. "We hung out together, shopped, talked about our kids, our husbands, smoked cigarettes and drank black coffee. Sometimes we wore each other's clothes. Betty and I were about the same size." At five feet seven inches, Betty was slightly taller than Rita but they both weighed around 130 pounds. Betty had reddish-brown hair that reached her shoulders; Rita's dark brown hair touched her waist. They each had high cheekbones, Betty's more pronounced than Rita's, and their eyes were large and a dark amber.

The bond between Rita and Betty was stronger than that of most friends. According to Rita's mother, Wanda Brookmyer, Rita spent considerable time with Betty's younger daughter, Linda.

"They were so close," Wanda said. "At times, the child called Rita her mother. Betty even considered letting Rita adopt Linda."

Rita later told me that she and Betty had discussed it. "Why do you think Betty told the police that she saw Richard hit Miley with a baseball bat at your trailer?" I asked.

Rita hesitated and shook her head, searching for an explanation. "I guess she was just trying to save herself. During the trial, Betty testified that the police threatened to take her kids."

"If you could talk with Betty today, what you would you say?"

Rita paused and seemed to plead as she spoke. "Why? Why did you do this to me? That's what I'd say."

"Do you feel a lot of anger towards Betty?"

"No." Rita stopped and chose each word carefully. "I don't hate her."

"How could you not hate someone who's responsible for you being in prison?"

"Maybe Betty's got a story to tell," Rita said. Her words became more defensive. "Maybe there are reasons she said what she did. Reasons we just don't know."

"Don't you think she should pay for what she did?" I asked.

Rita pondered the possibilities. "Oh, I guess I would like to see her spend maybe three or four years in prison. Just to see what it's like. But I wouldn't want anyone to go through what I've gone through."

Both Rita and Betty had experienced relationships with violent men. Neither had known the touch of a tender man. In their sameness, Rita and Betty felt a measure of safety; one looked out for the other. Maybe that's why Rita found Betty's testimony so shocking.

11   Washed Away by an April Rain

On the basis of the facts given at the trials, the Miley murder stretched the imagination. The cause of death was unknown; the murder weapon was in doubt. The state based a large part of its case on the testimony of Betty Boyer, who allegedly saw Richard Nitz hit Michael Miley in the head with a baseball bat. But to lend Boyer's story credibility, physical evidence was needed.

The state turned to forensics, the application of science to law, to provide physical evidence. The forensic scientist has an array of tools—fingerprinting, blood tests, examination of human tissue, and autopsy, to name a few—to support the state's case. And unlike an ordinary witness, forensic scientists, considered expert witnesses by the court, are allowed to offer opinions on their findings. Garnati, hoping to find some rock-hard evidence to support the state's claim, turned to three local forensic scientists. But after reading their testimony, I was left wondering.

David Michael Pittman Jr., a forensic scientist employed by the Illinois State Police, examined evidence from crime scenes for latent impressions. He described the underside of the human hand as having a unique surface called friction ridge skin. When this skin comes in contact with natural body fluids and oils or any foreign contaminant, such as motor oil or catsup, a replication of that particular area of the skin will be left on whatever surface it rests on. That is called a latent impression.

Pittman described the inked print as a recording of an individual's fingerprints. "It is done by placing a thin layer of printer's ink on the fingers and the fingers are rolled on a standard fingerprint card," said Pittman. Inked fingerprints of fifteen different people, including those of Rita Nitz, were given to Pittman to compare with latent impressions found on various exhibits from the crime scene.

> exhibit 24—a chrome trim from Michael Miley's car. Pittman found one latent impression that matched no one on the submitted list.
> exhibits 25 and 26—Two lifts, cards with latent impressions, taken from the crime scene matched Bill Woodis, a camper who discovered the body.
> exhibit 27—one lift that matched Bill Woodis
> exhibit 28—one lift that matched Brett Miles, a camper who discovered the body
> exhibit 46—one FM-AM cassette radio with two latent impressions that matched no one on the submitted list

When Drew asked Pittman whether he had examined the bat, the knife, and the shovel for fingerprints, Pittman answered no. Sounding surprised, Drew asked, "Is it customary when evidence is brought in from the same crime, that you would conduct a test on all of the related items?"

"Yes," Pittman answered. "Generally I would work on all of the items to be processed for latent prints in a particular case."

"Were you the only person doing fingerprints?" Drew asked.

"The only person doing fingerprints at the Carbondale laboratory," Pittman answered.

"Okay, so you didn't find Rita Nitz's prints on anything?" Drew asked. "None of the above, is that right?"

"That's correct," Pittman answered.

Glen Schubert, a forensic scientist employed by the Illinois State Police, performed microscopic examinations and comparisons of hair, fibers, soil, wood, safe insulation, building material, and unknown particles. Schubert commonly examines hairs in a case to determine whether they are human or animal. If human, Schubert determines the part of the body on which the hair originated—head, facial, or pubic—and the race of the person—Caucasian, Negroid, or Mongoloid.

> exhibit 19—a pair of blue jeans, a pair of underwear, a pair of socks, a pair of shoes, and a white handkerchief. Schubert observed four Caucasian pubic hairs and one Caucasian pubic hair fragment. All hairs were consistent with the pubic hair standard of Mike Miley. They were dissimilar to the pubic hair standards of Richard Nitz and Rita Nitz.
>
> exhibit 20A—pubic hair combings of Michael Miley. Schubert observed eighteen Caucasian pubic hairs and two Caucasian pubic hair fragments that were consistent with the pubic hair standard of Michael Miley. They were dissimilar to the pubic hair standards of Richard Nitz and Rita Nitz.
>
> exhibit 20C—debris from the pubic area of Michael Miley. Schubert observed two Caucasian pubic hairs that were consistent with the pubic hair standard of Michael Miley. They were dissimilar to the pubic hair standards of Richard Nitz and Rita Nitz.
>
> exhibit 22—cardboard slide containing a glass microscope slide. The glass slide contained a single hair found on the left wrist of Michael Miley. The hair was a Caucasian head hair fragment, and it was consistent with hairs from the hairbrush of Michael Miley. Schubert said the hair fragment was broken and appeared to be crushed. It was dissimilar to the hair standards of Richard Nitz and Rita Nitz.
>
> exhibit 50—baseball bat. No hairs were present on the baseball bat.

Upon cross-examination, Drew asked Schubert whether the debris found in the pubic hair of Michael Miley was unusual, particularly when the body was clothed. "Most often we do not see botanical material or particles," answered Schubert.

Andrew Wist, a forensic scientist employed by the Illinois State Police, worked in serology, the field of science used in the crime laboratory to analyze bodily fluids, such as blood, saliva, and semen.

> exhibit 19—one pair of blue jeans, a pair of socks, a pair of shoes, and a white handkerchief. Wist found human blood on the blue jeans and the white handkerchief. The blood was type O, which was not consistent with the blood of Richard Nitz and Rita Nitz, both of whom have type A.
>
> exhibit 20—sexual assault kit. No sperm cells were found on the rectal swab or the larynx swab of Michael Miley.

> exhibit 33—gold-colored Timex watch. Wist found specks of type O blood, inconsistent with the blood standard of Richard Nitz and Rita Nitz.
> exhibit 47—knife. Wist found traces of blood that proved to be nonhuman.
> exhibit 48—shovel. No blood, human tissue, or human hair was found on the shovel.
> exhibit 50—baseball bat. No blood, human tissue, or human hair was found on the surface of the bat.
> exhibit 72—Richard Nitz blood standard. Type A.
> exhibit 73—Rita Nitz blood standard. Type A.

Garnati suggested the likelihood that the baseball bat had been wiped clean or the weather had stripped it of any evidence. The bat was found in Richard Nitz's car. Robert Drew, unwilling to accept Garnati's premise, questioned Wist about the condition of the bat and the lack of blood, human tissue, and human hair.

"Now, the first test you did on the bat was a visual exam?" Drew asked.

"That's correct," Wist answered.

"If this bat had been washed or scrubbed," Drew said, "would you have been able to determine that from visually examining it?"

"Not necessarily," Wist said.

Drew, lifting the bat into the air, pointed out that it was dirty, the finish was nonexistent, and it appeared quite old. "Would you have been able to detect bleach or detergent if it had been present on the bat?" Drew asked.

"I don't know," Wist answered. "It would depend upon how it reacted to the bat. Like I said, I didn't see any visual signs that indicated to me that it had been washed."

"How long have you been involved in your current profession?" Drew asked.

"Fourteen years," Wist answered.

"Do you ordinarily find evidence of blood or hair or bits of matter related to the beating with a bat?" Drew asked.

"I have on some bats and some bats I haven't," Wist said.

"All right, Mr. Wist, would you tell the jury, sir, in your experience with baseball bats, if this baseball bat had been used to strike a human head, drawing blood, crushing the skull, would there be residue on the bat if it had been kept up in an automobile out of the weather?"

"If I received it relatively soon after the incident I would expect to find something on it," Wist said.

"Would there be some porosity or seepage into the interior of the wood?" Drew asked.

"There might be, yes," Wist answered. And when asked about the equipment used in his lab, Wist said, "I feel we use the best tests available at this point in time."

Drew picked up the bat and brought it to the witness chair. "Mr. Wist, would you do a visual examination of that bat right now? Is it not true that this bat does not appear to have been washed or scrubbed?"

"I don't see any signs that it has been scrubbed or washed," Wist answered.

"Okay, thank you, Mr. Wist. That's all."

Rita, age two, with her two older brothers, Kenneth *(right)* and Richard *(left)*.
Courtesy of Wanda Brookmyer.

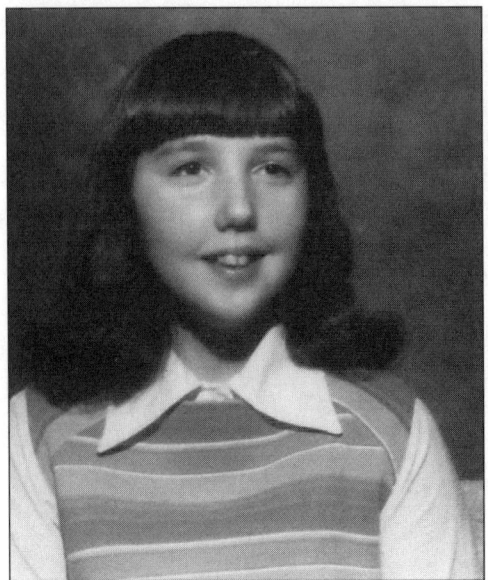
School photo of Rita, age eleven.
Courtesy of Wanda Brookmyer.

Rita in 1996, with the following written on the back of the photo: "Mom, Always know you are loved and appreciated tremendously. Yours forever, Rita Jo."
Courtesy of Wanda Brookmyer.

A 1997 photo sent to Rita's father with the following written on the back: "Dad, You have been a bigger influence in my life than you could ever know. You taught me what love is about and to hold on to faith. Thanks for everything. I love you! Rita Jo Brookmyer."
Courtesy of Wanda Brookmyer.

Rita in 1999, with the following message to her mother: "Mom, No words could ever express how much I love and miss you. I'm so thankful that you are my mother and I deeply appreciate all you do and are. Love forever and more, Rita Jo Brookmyer." Courtesy of Wanda Brookmyer.

Rita and her two training dogs, Rambler and Elliot, June 29, 2000.
Courtesy of Wanda Brookmyer.

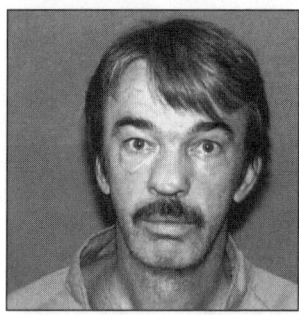

Richard Nitz.
Photo from the Illinois
Department of Corrections
Web site.

Michael Miley.
Courtesy of *Crimson and Corn*, Murphysboro High School yearbook (1982, vol. 63), Murphysboro, Illinois.

Front view of the Dwight Correctional Center. Courtesy of Anthony Thorsen.

12 Stains, Residue, and Blood Splatters

"I don't believe that Rita Nitz had anything to do with the death of Michael Miley." That is what Martin Edward Heischmidt, a professor of criminal justice at Rend Lake College, told me on November 30, 2001. Ed, as Heischmidt is known, had agreed to meet with me and discuss the Rita Nitz case. I believed that his testimony raised serious doubt about the credibility of Betty Boyer at Rita's trial.

"I wouldn't have worked on Rita's case if I had believed she was guilty," Ed said. "I know I get criticized for that, but that's how I feel." He went on to explain that after so many years in law enforcement, he cannot bring himself to work on a case when he believes the accused committed the crime. "I met with Rita on several occasions. I believe I've developed a certain intuition for determining whether someone is telling the truth. I look for facial expressions, the shifting or blinking of eyes, whether they seem anxious, all kinds of things." He laughed slightly. "It's not scientific, it's just a gut feeling, but I believed that Rita was innocent."

Ed, a tall, gray-haired, medium-skinned man with a neatly trimmed mustache, was dressed in blue jeans and a navy-blue sweater. His hair lacked a visible part, giving Ed an untidy but slightly rugged look. With only the hint of a double chin, he still was in good shape for someone who appeared to be in his fifties. Ed's enthusiasm for his work was evident as he talked, leaning forward and then backward and at times waving both arms to illustrate a point. Students walked down the hallway past his open door. We were at the North Oasis, a building at Rend Lake College.

"I realize it's been over twelve years since Rita's trial," I said. "I don't know how much you remember about the case."

"Oh, I remember it well," answered Ed. "The nature of the crime made it a high-profile case. And there was a lot of pressure placed on me."

"What kind of pressure?" I asked.

"The prosecution did everything they could to dig up some dirt on me."

"I don't understand," I said.

"The prosecution called the college and asked for my personnel file," Ed replied. "They called the college president, and they even called my former employer when I was a policeman in St. Louis and wanted to know why I left. They wanted to discredit me." He waved his arms and raised his voice. "I got telephone calls from the police telling me that I shouldn't testify for the defense. That I was part of the police family and that it was wrong to go against my fellow policemen."

A few seconds of silence passed as Ed waited for my response. "Oh, I'm sorry," I said. "I was just thinking. It's not that I don't believe you. It's just hard for me to accept that maybe the police and prosecutor don't always do the right thing. I was raised during a time when Jack Webb was a detective on *Dragnet* and Perry Mason was in the courtroom. It was easy to tell the good guys from the bad guys."

Ed chuckled. "Yes, I know what you mean. I was raised during those same years. But you better get used to it. There're good and bad people on both sides of the law."

There was a slight pause as Ed seemed to reflect. "There're a lot of problems with the legal system. We have people serving life for drug offenses, while others serve just a few years for rape. DNA testing is showing how we've put innocent people in prison." Ed paused again. "Yes, there's a lot of problems. I just tell my students to be good people and go out and do a good job."

Our discussion jumped back to Rita's trial in September 1989. Robert Drew called Heischmidt to the witness stand and went over the professor's accomplishments, hoping to establish him as an expert witness for the defense.

Beginning in 1968, Heischmidt was a uniformed patrol officer and then a plainclothes investigator of homicides, arson, rapes, robberies, and burglaries for the St. Louis Metropolitan Police Department. While working as a police officer, he attended the FBI academy, for training in crime scene investigations and high-risk incidents control, and the U.S. Army School at Huntsville, Alabama, for training in the handling of crime scenes that involve bombs and arson and in dignitary protection.

Heischmidt earned a social and applied science degree from the St. Louis Community College in 1974 and in 1976 received a bachelor's degree in political science and legal justice from Maryville College. In 1978 he earned a master's degree in constitutional law and American civil liberties from St. Louis University. When I talked with him, Heischmidt had completed eighteen hours past a master's degree at the college of criminal justice at Southern Illinois University. In addition, he had attended more than forty training seminars, ranging from eight hours to more than 120 hours as a crime scene technician in advanced fingerprint science, and a variety of other courses that dealt with crime scenes and evidence acquisitions.

He was the coordinator of the criminal justice program at Rend Lake College, the chairman of the Southern Illinois Criminal Justice Training Program, and a member of the International Association of Chiefs of Police and the Academy of Criminal Justice Sciences.

Even after Heischmidt's weighty qualifications were described, Garnati objected when Drew asked the court to recognize him as an expert witness. Hoping to lessen the impact of his testimony, Garnati attempted to portray him as a mere academic who sat behind a desk and lacked any hands-on experience, someone whose past police work had been spent issuing parking tickets. Throughout Garnati's cross-examination, Drew's objections were as rare as rain during a summer drought.

Finally, after Garnati had no more questions, he still objected to Heischmidt being called an expert witness. Judge Lowery ordered the jury from the courtroom. "Well, the statute is clear," Lowery said as he spoke to the two attorneys. "It says that an expert is a person who because of education, training, or experience possesses knowledge of a specialized nature beyond that of the average person on a factual matter material to a claim or a defense in pending litigation and who may be expected to render an opinion within his expertise at trial. Now, that sets forth by statutory definition in Illinois. The weight to be given to the testimony of an expert witness is the jury's decision. The primary finding is whether or not a witness who is offered as an expert has the particular training or skill beyond that of a layman."

The jury returned. "The court will come to order," Lowery said. "The witness is declared to be an expert in the field of crime scene technology. You may proceed."

It was the defense's belief that Betty Boyer's account of Richard Nitz's attack of Michael Miley was false. After all, Rita Nitz said that she was not present during the alleged attack and that Betty's story was created through the direction of the prosecution. And as a result, the defense chose to prove, through the lack of forensic evidence, that Betty's story had no substance. It was a lie.

Because of his expertise, Heischmidt was hired to reconstruct the alleged crime scene to determine whether Betty's story had merit. He made a detailed drawing of the crime scene, including the Nitz trailer, two cars, walk, concrete patio, trees, driveway, adjacent road, and Miley's car. The locations of the cars, Richard and Rita Nitz, and Michael Miley were based on testimony presented by Betty Boyer at the Richard Nitz trial. Betty Boyer had described the crime scene as she witnessed it through the window of the Nitzes' trailer on the evening of April 6, 1988.

Heischmidt looked through the living room window, searching for an angle that would yield the widest view of the crime scene. In addition, he took several photographs with a thirty-five-millimeter camera that were later used as a reference in reconstruction of the crime scene. Drew wanted to show that Boyer could not have seen Richard Nitz strike Miley with a baseball bat or, with the help of Rita, place Miley's body in the trunk of Miley's car.

Heischmidt sat in the witness chair. "I responded to the crime scene and from the most favorable vantage point inside the trailer I attempted to visualize the area in which most of her testimony was based, and found that even at the most advantageous point that it was extremely difficult or impossible to see the area." Boyer's account of the crime scene, as she previously testified at Richard's trial, was not plausible.

She could not have seen a body being loaded into the trunk of Miley's car, because the vehicle was not visible from the window where Boyer claimed to have stood.

On April 28, 1988, when detectives went to the Nitzes' trailer with a search warrant, Boyer had not yet told her story. There was no reason to believe that a crime had taken place at the trailer. Still, Frank Cooper, a crime scene investigator for the Illinois State Police, testified earlier that he made a thorough inspection of the premises. Since no signs of blood, human tissue, or hair fragments were seen, no scientific tests were performed to determine whether evidence had been absorbed into the concrete, gravel, or anywhere at the crime scene. Only a wooden baseball bat, a red-stained shovel, and a knife were seized as potential evidence.

On May 6, 1988, Boyer told the police that the crime had been committed outside the Nitzes' trailer. Richard Nitz was arrested, and five days later, so was Rita. Still the police did not go back to the crime scene and perform an additional search. Frank Cooper said that if anything had been at the Nitz trailer on April 28, he would have seen it. But the defense did not accept that premise. If Boyer's story were true, the defense believed, some evidence would have been at the crime scene and not entirely worn away by the elements of nature.

"Mr. Heischmidt," Drew said, "I would like to ask your expert opinion in terms of being a crime scene investigator. Assuming that someone had been brutally murdered with a baseball bat and struck numerous blows somewhere along the sidewalk and driveway area, and assume that these had been blows, several blows full force from behind the head, and assume that you were made aware of this one month from the day after the occurrence. What would be the first order of business for a crime scene technician?"

"I would visit the scene to see if there were any indicators to substantiate the alleged crime," Heischmidt said.

"What would you expect to find?" Drew asked.

"Well, the whole premise behind responding to the scene is that you search everywhere. There may be things left behind that were not of a fragile nature that could not have been destroyed. So, I would not have a preconceived notion. I would conduct a whole systematic search of the complete environment, hoping to enlighten myself about the alleged crime."

"Is that what you teach police officers, to secure the area and conduct a full crime scene examination?" Drew asked.

"Yes," Heischmidt answered.

"Is there any reason why that would not have been done, given the facts that I have alluded to?" Drew asked.

"No," Heischmidt replied.

"Do you have an opinion as to the failure of the officer in charge to order that done?" Drew asked.

"Well," Heischmidt said. "Starting in an academy and throughout a police career, the timely crime scene investigation is considered so important that to fail to avail oneself of the evidential potential would be looked on, in the best sense, as an error in judgment and, in the worst sense, probably as malpractice."

Drew asked Heischmidt for his opinion about the amount of blood spattering that would be generated by the wielding of a baseball bat in the manner described in Betty Boyer's testimony: two or three or four times while the victim was standing and then two or three times after Miley had fallen to the ground.

"In our laboratory at the college, we have four human skulls that are part of our teaching exhibits," Heischmidt said. "One of those human skulls was dropped one time by one of the students, and it shattered. I have measured the bone width of those skulls and the anterior portion of the human skull is approximately . . ."

"Let me stop you there, Mr. Heischmidt. For my benefit and probably for the jurors, would you tell us what anterior means?"

"The front, the anterior of this bone being the front bone, and the posterior is the rear, and the temporal would be the sides. The bone width is thickest, perhaps, one-half inch in the back. They are much less thick, approximately three-eighths, in front and only one-eighth inch thick in the temporal regions. I base that on actual measurements. The use of a normal wood baseball bat coming in contact with the skull could not only break the tissue but it could destroy the bone, it could shatter the entire cranial area, exposing the brain and perhaps even knocking the brain from the cranial area."

When asked to describe the baseball bat, Heischmidt said it was an older wooden bat without a protective finish, and the handle was wrapped in duct tape. Other than that, it appeared to be normal.

"After your examination, if that bat had been used in the type of incident that I have just described, would it show signs or would there be any porosity, blood, or other matter reflected?"

"Yes," Heischmidt said. "That is an excellent possibility of a violent crime."

"Okay, getting to splatters and patterns, could you render an opinion based upon your expertise as to what kind of damage this type of attack would create, given the dimensions and the place?" Drew asked.

"The bat is a sturdy object and there appears to be no rot and it is not cracked," Heischmidt said. "I think it is fully capable, if wielded in the hands of any individual, if struck about the head area, that not only hair, flesh, bone, brain matter, and copious amounts of blood would attach to it, but in the forward motions blood splatters would permeate the area. In the rearward motions, as someone comes back, the blood attached to it would cause it, the primary secondary force, to have blood splattered in nearly a three hundred and sixty-degree circle from the assault."

"Okay," Drew said. "Based on your expert opinion, if the incident happened anywhere along the length or width of this trailer, would it be highly probable or improbable, that matter, stains, residue, blood splatters would attach to the mobile home?"

"I think it is highly probable that they would," Heischmidt said.

"What about up under the eaves of the protected area?" Drew asked.

"I think that is likely as well," Heischmidt answered.

"Now Mr. Heischmidt, let me call your attention again to the concrete, which is depicted in that photograph. Did you have occasion to visually examine that concrete?"

"Yes sir," Heischmidt replied. "I visually examined the sidewalk and the concrete area."

"Okay, did you find any evidence of bloodstains or residue?" Drew asked.

"No, I did not," Heischmidt answered.

"Are you familiar with the concepts of the porosity of concrete?" Drew asked.

"Yes," Heischmidt said.

"Could you give the jury an example of what you mean?" Drew asked.

"We are talking about the absorption quality of concrete and if anything that would meet the surface of concrete would leave a stain,"

Heischmidt answered. "I am familiar with concrete's ability to leave stains."

"Would an oil spot in the middle of an otherwise clean driveway be consistent with the type of stain that you are talking about?" Drew asked.

"Yes, sir, it would," Heischmidt replied.

"In your experience, Mr. Heischmidt, and based on your expertise in laboratory work, would the amount of blood generated by an attack of this nature have left a bloodstain on the concrete driveway or sidewalk?"

"Yes, it would," Heischmidt answered.

"Can you render an opinion as to whether or not that bloodstain, after having been there in a substantial amount of blood as you have indicated, after having laid there for several hours through the nighttime hours, could be washed away or scrubbed away?"

"I think it would be a difficult process," Heischmidt said. "There is a possibility that it could be completely obliterated, yes, sir."

"Well, would it be good practice for the crime scene people had they arrived to check those matters?" Drew asked.

"Yes, it would," Heischmidt answered.

"Especially if they were given a particular location as to where it occurred?" Drew asked.

Again, Heischmidt answered, "Yes, sir."

Heischmidt's speculation as to the shattered skull and the flying blood and human tissue seemed logical if Miley was hit five or six times with a baseball bat. The murder of a Massachusetts woman as reported on *All Things Considered* (National Public Radio), on December 20, 1993, yielded similar results. Early one Sunday morning, Franke Galuf walked downstairs from his bedroom and discovered his sister, Kathy Robbins, lying on the living room couch. "All I could see was a lot of the blood on the ceiling, on the walls. I saw the baseball bat on the floor." Kathy was beaten to death by her husband, Steven Robbins. Another death by a baseball bat was reported by Raquel Exner in the *Edmonton* [Alberta] *Sun*. Exner described Leif Lundgren Sr. walking into his son's apartment one morning and seeing his son lie motionless on the floor with a blanket partially covering his head. "I pulled the blanket off his face. There was a hole where his left eye was. There was blood on the carpet and a baseball bat by his head."

If Miley had been hit with such frequency and force, it is unlikely that he would have survived. Still, earlier testimony from pathologist Dr. Beverly Tsai revealed that Miley's lungs were pinkish red, indicating traces of carbon monoxide. This finding would suggest that Miley was alive when he was placed in the trunk of his car.

During the cross-examination, Garnati and Heischmidt volleyed back and forth as to the relevancy and accuracy of Heischmidt's crime scene reconstruction. Garnati attempted to diminish Heischmidt's testimony on the premise that a traumatized person's memory is flawed. And as a result, while Betty Boyer's testimony might be inaccurate as to the location of the cars and Miley's body, it did not mean that Boyer was lying.

Garnati said that Heischmidt's experiments with human skulls were of no value, since the skulls in his lab were old and lacked skin, tissue, and human hair. And in all likelihood, Miley's head would not have shattered as Heischmidt had speculated.

Phillip K. Sylvester, a sergeant with the Illinois State Police, was recalled to the stand. On the previous day, the prosecution had directed Sylvester to go to the Nitzes' trailer and perform a reconstruction of the crime scene. Since Boyer's earlier testimonies had varied as to the exact location of the cars and Miley's body, he used an approximation or an average as to where each item of the crime scene was located. Naturally, the results differed from Heischmidt's testimony. On the basis of Sylvester's reconstruction, it would have been possible for Boyer to have seen what she described from the living room window.

After reading the testimonies concerning the crime scene, I can only wonder how Betty Boyer could have seen anything through the living room window. Except for a porch light and a vapor light on an elevated pole, it was dark outside. Boyer, who testified that without glasses her vision was fuzzy, was not wearing glasses when she looked out the window that night. A love seat, a bookshelf, an end table and a lamp were in the living room. The lit lamp sat on the end table and was no more than a few feet from the window. When asked whether the glare from the lamp caused problems in seeing the crime scene, Betty answered no. When asked whether she put her hands on the glass to shut out the light, Betty answered no.

Hoping to measure Betty's visibility, I tried to recreate the scene at my home. When I looked out my living room window while a lit lamp sat on an end table and the porch light was on, I saw my faint reflection. Only by using my hands to shut out the light from my lamp could

I see anything. If no forensic evidence was found at the alleged crime scene, maybe no crime was committed at the Nitz trailer.

As our meeting came to a close, Heischmidt seemed somewhat troubled. "Sometimes I wonder if I did a poor job in presenting my testimony," he said. "Maybe I was too technical. Maybe if I had said it in a different way, Rita wouldn't be in jail."

"I thought your testimony was clear," I said. "I don't believe that was the problem. Why do you think the jury found Rita guilty?"

"Well, I wasn't there for the entire trial. Since I was a witness, I could only attend when I was on the stand. But from what I did see, the trial seemed out of balance."

"What do you mean?" I asked.

"If the judicial system is to work properly, each side needs to present its case with equal determination and enthusiasm. I don't think that was the case with this trial. Rita's defense didn't seem to have the commitment. As a result, Garnati was free to do whatever he wanted."

13 Stool Pigeon, Squealer, and Snitch

A short, full-bodied woman at five feet and 150 pounds, Barbara Winkler stood with her right hand on the Bible and swore "to tell the truth and nothing but the truth." Winkler, a hardened nineteen-year-old with black hair, brown eyes, and medium skin, said that she had dropped out of high school after completing her freshman year and admitted to frequent struggles with the law. A witness for the state, Winkler was serving time in the Logan Correctional Facility at Lincoln, Illinois.

In 1988 Winkler was arrested in Arkansas for driving a stolen vehicle and was extradited to Williamson County to undergo trial for nine counts of forgery. In 1989 Winkler was arrested in Nebraska for driving a stolen car and was extradited to Williamson County for theft of a vehicle. Alex Fine, a public defender in Williamson County, testified that he had represented Barbara Winkler on cases of vehicle theft and forgery. Fine said that after plea bargaining, Barbara Winkler agreed to plead guilty to the theft charges and to accept a three-year sentence. In exchange, the nine counts of forgery were dropped and Winkler received credit for the seventy-six days she had served in the

Williamson County Jail. Winkler later testified that she received a good deal from the state's attorney's office.

Rita and Barbara shared a cell at the Williamson County Jail from March 7, 1989, to April 26, 1989. Winkler claimed that Rita made her write a letter that contained statements allegedly made by Betty Boyer, a witness for the prosecution. "Rita said that if I didn't write what she said, then her gang would get me when I'm out." Winkler added that Robert Drew would make sure that her kids were taken away from her. According to the letter, Betty Boyer and Richard Nitz were responsible for Michael Miley's death and Rita was set up by the two of them. Winkler said that everything in the letter was false.

"Rita told me that her and Richard beat this guy with a baseball bat and shot him in the head and hung him from a tree." Winkler said that she could not remember many details of the beating. Still she claimed that Rita repeated the story some twenty or thirty times a day.

"When you and Rita were in the Williamson County Jail, were all of the cells being used?" Drew asked.

"Yes," Winkler replied.

"Does that mean there were six girls there at all times?" Drew asked.

"Yes," Winkler answered.

"So the other girls would have heard any conversations that you had with Rita?" Drew questioned.

"Yes," Winkler answered.

"Are you telling this jury the truth and whole truth about every bit of this?" Drew asked.

Again, Winkler answered, "Yes."

Rita's story was quite different. She said that when Barbara Winkler was placed in her cell in March 1989, she was told that since she had been in the Williamson County Jail for nearly one year, she was to show Barbara the ropes. Rita went on to explain that they got along fine until photographs of her nephew and niece were missing. At the time, Rita was unaware that Barbara had sent the photos with a letter to a male inmate, telling him that they were her children. Days later, the male inmate returned the photos to Barbara. Although Barbara denied any knowledge of the photos, Rita complained to Lieutenant Karen Clark and Officer Cindy Olson, guards at the Williamson County jail. A shakedown was conducted in the cell block, and the photos were found in Barbara's jumpsuit.

"Barbara and the other women prisoners believed that I was innocent," Rita told me. I found, in a court file, letters written by Deborah Williams, Jari Pollard, Karen Allen, and Delores Simpson, all inmates of the Williamson County Jail, saying that Rita had maintained her innocence throughout her incarceration and that she was a caring person. "The photo incident angered Barbara," Rita added, "and she lashed out by denying the contents of the letter."

Later I asked Rita why Drew did not have the other inmates testify, since they were in agreement with her story. "He was afraid to," Rita answered. "Drew said that if he asked them to testify, then Garnati might get to them and they could change their story. He said we couldn't take the risk of Garnati making deals with them, too."

The use of a jailhouse informant in Rita's trial was not unique. Throughout history, the use of informants to prove or build on the prosecutor's case has been common. The state's use of Winkler was no different. Societal demands to escalate the war on drugs spurred an increase in the use of informants, and it has generally been accepted as a means to plug the holes in a dam that blocks the flow of drugs into the country. In many cases, it has been successful. Scores of criminals have been prosecuted because of the truthful testimony of informants.

But, as many point out, our liberal use of informants threatens our legal system. "Throughout the country," Mark Curriden wrote in the *National Law Journal*, "law enforcement's reliance on informants has grown to almost Orwellian proportions, as snitches exert growing control over agents, and judges fail to impose any checks or balances." One does not have to look hard for the reasons why prosecutors depend so much on the testimony of snitches. It's easier. Reliance on the snitch has replaced good, solid police work. Some would argue that prosecutors are driven by their winning percentages to the point of allowing the ends to justify the means.

Judge Stephen S. Trott, the chief of the criminal division of the Reagan Justice Department, told the *Hastings Law Journal* that informants are likely to say or do anything to have their sentences reduced. "This willingness to do anything includes not only truthfully spilling the beans on friends and relatives, but also lying, committing perjury, manufacturing evidence, soliciting others to corroborate their lies with more lies and double-crossing anyone with whom they come into contact, including—and especially—the prosecutor." And E. Michael McCann, the chairman of the American Bar Association's criminal justice section, agrees that the more informants are used, the more potential there is for abuse.

According to the Death Penalty Information Center in Washington, DC, since 1988 seven death row inmates in five states—Arkansas, California, Florida, Georgia, and Texas—have had their convictions reversed after it was learned that informants had lied to the jury, that police officers had pressured snitches to fabricate jailhouse confessions, or that prosecutors had failed to disclose payments to informants.

Willie Rainge was twice sentenced to life in prison for murder and rape. In each trial, as Lawrence C. Marshall, a professor of law at Northwestern University, explains, the prosecution used the testimony of informants. Some ten years after the 1978 trial, the jailhouse informant who testified that he overheard Rainge acknowledge killing the victim admitted that in exchange for his testimony, he was spared a lengthy prison sentence. At the time of Rainge's 1987 trial, the informant was gone, but another individual, Paula Gray, testified that she witnessed the crimes. In return, her murder charges were dropped. In 1996, after eighteen years of incarceration, Rainge was found innocent of all charges and was granted his freedom.

And in Rolando Cruz's 1990 trial, the prosecutors presented as a witness a death row inmate who testified that he had once heard Cruz admit to killing Jeanine Nicarico. Lawrence Marshall, in an essay called "What Do We Owe People Who Have Been Wrongly Convicted?," explains that the state, having taken the position that the informant had lied about his own case and deserved execution, was willing to ask a jury to execute Cruz on the basis of the informant's word. In 1995, DuPage County judge Ronald Mehling found the former death row inmate innocent because the initial murder investigation had been "sloppy, very sloppy" and the government's case against Cruz was riddled with lies and mistakes.

Concern over the use of informants, particularly those with a sordid past, is growing. As John Gorrell, a *Free Press* contributor, adds, "the loose tongue, the braggadocio and the snitch are priceless tools of law enforcement. It's the use of the informer, the fink, the stool-pigeon, squealer and snitch that requires scrutiny in a society whose civil rights are under pressure as never before.... Informers either have 'axes to grind,' their butts are in the wringer with the criminal laws, or they lust after the largesse that comes with snitching." Gorrell believes that prosecutors have free reign in their use of informants and, as a result, have little fear of the federal bribery statute, 18 S.C. 201©)(2), which reads, "Whoever directly or indirectly gives, offers or promises anything of value to any person for testimony before any court shall be fined or imprisoned for not more than two years, or both."

Standing alone, Barbara Winkler's testimony against Rita was weak and probably had little effect on the jury. After all, this informant was in jail, had a record of criminal activity, and had an opportunity to have her sentence reduced. But when added to other allegations, the testimony gained a cumulative effect that tended to blur the truth.

14 Trogette

Throughout Rita's trial, Garnati talked about the Trog Club. "Richard Nitz, and this is going to sound strange to you, but it's true, Richard Nitz formed this club in Williamson County, and he called it the Trog Club. T-R-O-G. Richard Nitz was the leader of the Trog Club. He was called the head Trog. Under the leadership of Richard Nitz this Trog Club evolved into a group of people that would go out around the Crab Orchard Lake area in Williamson County to harass and intimidate homosexuals who would gather out there at certain spots to socialize. Now, how does Rita Nitz fit into this world of homosexuals? You will see that Rita Nitz, as I said, was married to Richard Nitz at that time. She was a member of this Trog Club Richard Nitz formed. In fact, you are going to see that she was also known as the Trogette, the woman Trog leader, if you can believe that, but it is true."

Garnati made the Trog Club sound like a gang: an organized group of criminals, hoodlums, or wrongdoers. The intent was clear. Gangs are often actively involved in drugs and weapons, and their presence instills fear. To be associated with or, more important, to be the coleader of such a group was bad. Imagine a gang of some fifteen to twenty members riding across the countryside on motorcycles, particularly late at night, when their activities were hidden from the general public: a gang, armed with ice picks, chains, and baseball bats, that harassed gay men. I can only wonder whether the jury pictured Rita as someone clothed in black leather straddling her Yamaha 650 Special as her long, dark hair trailed in the wind.

Charles Brookmyer, Rita's brother and a key witness for the prosecutor, helped substantiate the state's assertions about the Trog Club. Charles testified that the Trog Club was a group of fifteen to twenty people who rode motorcycles and harassed homosexuals, a club in which Richard was called Trog and Rita was called Trogette. Charles admitted being a member of the group but said he quit when he did not approve of their activities. When asked how Rita felt about homosexuals, Charles said, "I'm not sure how she felt. I did not see her object. You know, because Rick didn't like them I assumed she didn't."

Charles continued, saying that Richard was the leader and the members, including Rita, followed Richard's instructions. And when asked about Rita's role in the club, Charles said, "If anything happened to Rick, she was to take over."

Trog territory, as Charles Brookmyer described it, included a series of four parking lots within a mile or two of the Nitz trailer. One of those lots was where Richard and Rita were married. It was a place where Richard went to meditate and to meet with his friends for a cookout or to drink some beer; a place where some members of the male homosexual community met.

"Did Richard or Rita Nitz ever show their dislike for the homosexuals being out in the Trog territory?" Garnati asked.

"Yes," Charles answered.

"How would they do that?" Garnati asked.

"Go out to Trog territory and run them off," Charles said.

Rita sat in disbelief as her youngest brother, someone she helped raise, testified that his sister was Trogette, the coleader of a vicious club. Garnati finished his questioning. Robert Drew stood and began his cross-examination.

"All right," Drew said. "Let's talk about the Trogs here for a minute. I think you said there were fifteen or twenty people involved in this club?"

"Yes," Charles replied.

"Did you hold any position in the club?" Drew asked.

"No," Charles answered.

"What did you have to do to get in?" Drew asked.

"It was just a group of friends in the club," Charles said.

"A group of friends and you didn't have to do anything to get in," Drew said.

"Well, we had an initiation," Charles said. "I had to cut my hair. I had a tail."

"Do you know where the name Trog came from?" Drew asked.

"I'm not for sure," Charles said. "I know that I had heard of Trog before. We decided to call him Trog, myself and a few friends called him Trog."

"What did it mean?" Drew asked.

"It was short for Troglodyte," Charles replied. "It is like a prehistoric man or a caveman."

"Why did you choose that name to designate your future or present brother-in-law?" Drew asked.

"It seemed to fit," Charles said.

"Would it be fair to say then that the name came about as kind of a joke on Richard?

"Yes," Charles said.

"Wasn't it really just a group of people, a flexible loose group of people that got together periodically to party and involve themselves in activities out there at the lake?" Drew asked.

"Not just at the lake," Charles said. "It had started as a group of family and friends that partied together and ran around together and drove motorcycles together and just did things together."

"Who gave Rita the name Trogette?" Drew asked.

"That I'm not sure," Charles said. "I heard Rick call her that a few times."

"Wasn't that more or less just a joking reference to the fact that she was married to the Troglodyte?" Drew asked.

"Yes," Charles said.

"So it did not have any significance in and of itself, did it?" Drew asked.

"No," Charles said.

Rita and I sat at a small, circular table in the visit room at the Dwight Correctional Center. A half-empty Diet Pepsi sat in front of Rita, a Coke sat in front of me. An empty pretzel bag sat in the center. "What about the Trog Club?" I asked.

Rita looked down, as she picked at the label on the Pepsi bottle. "There was no Trog Club," she answered in a disgusted tone.

"What about your brother's testimony?" I asked. "Charles Brookmyer testified that there was a Trog Club. I thought that his testimony hurt your case. Was he lying?"

"Yes," Rita hesitated. "There's some things you need to understand. Things aren't always as they appear." Rita explained that Charles and her mother, Wanda Brookmyer, were always fighting. Things were so bad that when Charles was fifteen, he moved in with Rita. It was during this time when Rita returned to her trailer and discovered that her pickup truck was missing. Since Charles said he did not know what happened to the truck, she called the police and reported the truck as stolen. Days later, the truck was found abandoned in the ditch of a backcountry road. A local farmer said he saw Charles and two young men drive the truck into the ditch. After Charles admitted that he had taken the truck, Rita went to the sheriff and asked to withdraw the charges. It was too late. Charles was placed on three years' probation for a stolen vehicle.

Rita believed that Charles's probation and the fear of going to jail influenced her brother to tell Garnati what he wanted to hear. Wanda shared Rita's view. She claimed that Charles was afraid of Garnati and lied to keep himself out of jail. After all, Charles was only nineteen and had admitted to having carried weapons, getting into fights, drinking illegally, and doing a host of things that cause problems for someone on probation.

Rita's first attorney, Larry Beard, told me that there was no such club. He explained that it was just a group of friends who got together socially.

"Calling Richard a Trog was just a joke," Larry said. "It meant nothing."

Mike Wright, a Baptist minister and Richard's friend, laid claim to coming up with Richard's nickname, Troglodyte. During Wright's testimony at Richard's trial, Wright said that he and a friend were doing some body work on a car. Across the road, Richard Nitz—hot, sweaty, and with dirty hair reaching his shoulders—used a tree limb to beat the crinkled bumper on his car. Wright remembered laughing and telling his friend how Richard looked like a cave man—a Troglodyte—as he beat the hell out of that car with the tree limb. From then on, the name Troglodyte, or Trog for short, stuck with Richard.

Roy Dulaney, one of Rita's best friends from 1980 to 1989, was somewhat amused when I asked him about the Trog Club. "There was no such club," Roy said. "It was just a big joke. A group of six or eight people spent a lot of time just sitting around drinking coffee at Denny's and Wendy's in Carbondale. There was certainly no motorcycle gang. Only Richard and Rita had motorcycles. I didn't even have a car. Sometimes we met at someone's house or at Crab Orchard Lake for a cookout."

Roy explained that somebody bought a miniature doll, called a Troll, that could be attached to a key chain. The Troll had long, straight black hair and, in a funny sort of way, looked like Richard. From there, someone suggested that since the doll looked like a Trog—a prehistoric caveman—Richard should be called Trog.

"Richard loved being the center of attention," Roy said. "Sometimes he called Rita a Trogette. It was just a joke. Nothing more."

I could not help but wonder why Beard, Dulaney, and Wright were not asked to testify at Rita's trial about the significance of *Trog*. When I asked Rita, she looked down, shrugged her shoulders, and said, "I don't know."

15 Victim or Murderer?

Robert Drew had to decide whether Rita should take the stand. The state was obligated to prove her guilt beyond a reasonable doubt, and the heart of their case rested on Betty Boyer's testimony, which was weak at best. Still, Rita's not taking the stand might suggest guilt. She had been incarcerated in the Williamson County Jail for sixteen months, was on and off antidepressants, and as a result, might have been unstable. Putting her on the stand was risky.

But no one was prepared for what Drew would do. Rita was called as a witness to testify on her own behalf, was duly sworn in, and was asked the following by Drew: "Miss Brookmyer, were you at the Kentucky Oaks Mall with Richard Nitz on April 7 and 8 of 1988?"

"Yes," she said, "he made me go with him."

"Did you participate in any way in the death of Michael Miley?" Drew asked.

"No, I did not," she answered.

"Thank you, your Honor," Drew said. "I have no further questions."

I can only guess at the surprise experienced by everyone who sat in the Massac County courtroom that September day when Drew uttered

"I have no further questions." Perhaps the air was sucked from the room, leaving a vacuum of silence that was interrupted by worried whispers that whirled about. Drew and Garnati approached the bench, and the jury left the room. A muffled exchange ensued, and then the judge instructed Drew to put his motion on the record.

"Your honor," Drew said, "if it please the Court, we would move *in limine* that the State's Attorney not be allowed to cross-examine beyond the scope of direct examination."

A motion *in limine* is a request by the prosecutor or defense attorney that the court make a decision before the testimony begins. In this instance, Drew made a strategic move to place severe limitations on Garnati's cross-examination. Drew recalled two times when the court had exercised such restrictions during prior testimony: when Drew questioned a police officer and when Garnati questioned Ron Roach. On both occasions, the court limited the scope of questioning. Drew, in support of his motion, cited *McCormick on Evidence,* third edition, 1984, chapter 4, page 52; *Speez v. People Case,* 122 Il. App.; and *Hunter's Handbook,* a reference book for attorneys.

Seemingly disturbed by Drew's tactic, Garnati expressed confidence that the court was aware of the law on the scope of cross-examination. "This is not some new brilliant theory that Mr. Drew has come up with here at the last minute," Garnati said. "The question obviously is, based on what she has testified to from the witness stand, how far can I go." Garnati believed that the questions asked during the direct examination were very open, giving him a broad latitude. After all, Drew asked Rita whether she went to the Kentucky Oaks Mall with Richard on April 7 and 8 and Rita had answered by saying, "Yes, he made me go with him." This, in Garnati's opinion, gave him the option to discuss Miley's credit cards and whether Rita was forced to go with him. The question "Did you participate in any way in the death of Michael Miley?" was quite open. Garnati believed that this statement raised the question of Rita's credibility.

Drew attempted to bolster his motion by referring the court to prior cases that supported limits on cross-examination: Goodman, *Illinois Trial Evidence,* subsection 1103, "Scope of Cross Examination," and the cases of *People v. King,* 276 Il. 138; *Champion v. Knasiak,* 25 Il. App. 3d 192; and finally, *Ryan v. Monson,* 33 Il. App. 2d 406. Simply stated, each case declared that cross-examination is limited to matters brought out during direct examination.

The judge gave his ruling. "The purpose of cross-examination is to clarify the testimony which the witness gave on direct examination, and to test the witness's ability to observe, recall, and retell the events about which he testified, and to examine any bias that the witness may have in respect to the events about which she testified or he testified. The question, 'Did you participate in any way in the death of Michael Miley,' opens it up for cross-examination about her conduct on those nights because it is an open question. So, my ruling is that your motion *in limine* is denied in part and it is granted in part. You can ask her questions on cross-examination. . . . But I am not going to allow you to go into all of these collateral issues about letters in the jail and stuff like that. You can deal with the participation or nonparticipation of this witness in the death of Michael Miley. Bring the jury back in."

The defense had gambled and lost. In time they would know whether Rita could withstand the barrage of questions from the prosecution and whether the jury would perceive her to be a victim or a murderer.

Garnati began his cross-examination, asking Rita to describe her activities on the night of the murder. She said that her twelve-year-old son, Chucky, was sick and except for a trip to the emergency room to obtain some medication, the two of them spent the day at her trailer. At six p.m. they went to Chuck Hooker's trailer in Murphysboro to do their laundry. Richard joined them later. At eight thirty the three of them left Hooker's and went to the Veach gas station behind the Carbondale mall. There Rita sat in the car while Richard walked inside and visited with Hooker, who was working at the gas station that night. Minutes later Richard returned to the car, and they went to Rita's trailer, arriving between nine thirty and ten p.m. Rita took Chucky inside, gave him his medication, and sent him to bed.

"Richard was upset that Earlene hadn't returned his car," Rita said. "He walked to her trailer and came back around 10:30 p.m." She explained that after Richard found the car and discovered it was out of gas, he came back to the trailer, borrowed five dollars for gas money, and returned again around eleven p.m. Minutes later Richard left and returned in the early morning, after Rita had fallen asleep on the couch and the television screen was a sea of snow.

"His knock on the door startled me," she said. "It must have been 2 or 3 in the morning." Richard's car was stuck, and he asked her to pull him out. At first she refused, saying that Chucky was sick and she could not leave him. But the argument grew and, like many times before, escalated to screams, causing Chucky to awake from a medicated sleep. She gave way to Richard's demands and told Chucky that she would return in a few minutes.

Rita's testimony shaped an image of Richard walking to the garage, carrying a set of chains, and throwing them into the trunk of her car; the two of them drove to a remote area just down Spillway Road, where the sky was overcast and a light southwesterly breeze blew across an open field cut by a narrow road. The night was lit by two pairs of headlights: one from Rita's Plymouth Barracuda and another from Richard's beat-up car stuck in a rain-soaked ditch. Richard used the chains to connect the two cars and pull his car from the ditch.

"What happened out there?" Garnati asked.

"He unhooked my car, and I went to turn around," Rita replied. "As I drove by, he stopped me." She recalled seeing a wet spot on the ground and asking whether his car had a leak. She thought the oil pan had scraped on something when they pulled his car out. He said it was not oil; it was blood.

"Richard Nitz told you it was blood?" Garnati asked.

"Yes, he did," she answered.

"All right," Garnati said. "What did you do next?"

"I thought he had been out deer hunting or something," Rita said. While he kicked dirt over the spot and continued to talk, she noticed a pile of leaves across from the wet spot, on the other side of the road. It looked like the end of a pair of jeans sticking from a pile of leaves.

"A pile of leaves in April?" Garnati asked. "In early April?"

"It was a pile of leaves."

"Okay, go ahead," Garnati said.

"He asked me if I had ever seen a dead body," she said.

"So you saw something that might have been a puddle of blood and you saw something that appeared to be a body lying in some leaves?" Garnati asked.

"When I first saw the pile of leaves," Rita said, "I didn't think anything about it."

"And did you see another strange vehicle there?" Garnati asked.

"When I turned around I saw what appeared to be part of a vehicle," Rita replied.

"All right, you had no idea whose vehicle that was, correct?" Garnati asked.

"I didn't know," she answered.

"So, you had something that might have been a puddle of blood, you had a strange vehicle out there, and you had something that you are not really sure but might have been somebody's leg or not, and you didn't get suspicious at all?"

At the time, Rita said she was not suspicious. In January, when Richard told her he had killed someone, her attorney said that Richard was just trying to frighten her. She thought this was more of the same.

Garnati moved between the night of the murder, April 6, and the evenings of April 7 and 8, when Rita accompanied Richard to the Paducah mall. As I read the trial transcript, I wondered whether the back-and-forth movement was meant to confuse the witness, to trip her up, and to elicit some admission of guilt, or whether the prosecution wanted to confuse the jury so details would be forgotten and replaced by an illusion of guilt. Whatever the reason, the defense employed the same technique on several occasions.

Rita testified that at seven thirty p.m., or maybe eight, on the evening of April 7, 1988, she accompanied Richard to the shopping mall in Paducah, Kentucky. He came by her trailer and told her that they were going to Paducah to repossess a car that he was selling to Chuck Hooker. Richard and Rita made the one-hour trip to the mall in Rita's Plymouth Barracuda, and when they arrived, he walked to the passenger side and told her to get out, that he had some things to do.

"Okay, Miss Brookmyer, you voluntarily got out of the car, is that correct?"

"I got out of the car," she said. "I did not kick, fight or holler, no."

"All right, you wanted to go into the mall with him, didn't you?" Garnati said.

"I didn't want to go anywhere with him," Rita replied.

"There was a lot of people around that Paducah Mall, wasn't there?" Garnati asked.

"At the time that he pulled in there I didn't see anybody," she said. "I believed the mall was either closed or closing at the time that we pulled up."

"When you got into the mall and walked in there," Garnati said, "I'll bet there were some people in the mall, weren't there?"

"When I first got in the mall I didn't see anybody I knew," she answered.

Rita told me, some fourteen years after the incident, during one of my visits to the Dwight Correctional Center, that being questioned by

Garnati was like fighting off a pit bull. It was not what she wanted. From the beginning, she asked for a chance to tell her story. But Drew told her it had not worked for Richard and he had a different strategy, one that left her in a defensive stance, trying to survive Garnati's attack.

"All right, Garnati asked. "How far did you have to go before you saw your first person in the mall?"

"I believe it would have been the Penney's store," Rita replied.

"And that's a pretty big store, isn't it?" Garnati asked.

"I don't know how big it is," she said.

"The store was not closed when you went in there, was it?" Garnati asked.

"It looked as if they had been closing," Rita said. "There weren't any other customers."

"The question was, was the store closed when you went in there?" Garnati asked.

"It wasn't locked, no," Rita answered.

"And there were still clerks on duty, is that correct?" Garnati asked.

"I only saw one," Rita answered.

"Okay, while you were walking through Sears you did not look at any other part of the store to see if anybody else was in there?" Garnati asked.

"I wasn't at Sears, sir," Rita replied.

"Where were you at?" Garnati asked.

"Penney's," Rita said.

"Okay," Garnati said. "When you were at Penney's did you look and see if anybody else was in the store?"

"I didn't see anyone, no," Rita said.

"Were you still being forced at this time to go into the J. C. Penney's store with Richard Nitz?" Garnati asked.

"I would call it force," Rita said. "It was a choice of either be there or be deserted somewhere, where I didn't know."

Since Rita previously admitted to having gone to the Paducah mall with Richard, Garnati's questioning focused on portraying her as a willing passenger rather than someone under duress. The jury was given a choice: Was Rita a battered woman, reacting out of fear for her life, or was she a loving wife wanting to please her husband?

Without an occasional objection from her attorney, Rita was left with little protection. Each question seemed to elicit her anger, churning up tension between Rita and Garnati like a strong undercurrent.

The bickering continued while he questioned her about the Ace bandages Richard wore at the Paducah mall.

"All right, those bandages, you have seen me pull those bandages out of one of the exhibits and show them to several witnesses, haven't you?" Garnati asked.

"I don't know that those are the same," Rita said. "I saw you show bandages earlier, yes."

"Okay, those bandages were found in your trailer, is that correct?" Garnati asked.

"I don't know that," Rita said. "I don't know what they took from there."

"Okay, Miss Brookmyer, they look very similar to the bandages that Richard Nitz had wrapped around his hands on April the 7th, isn't that correct?"

"All Ace bandages look the same," Rita said.

"I'm not asking you about all Ace bandages," Garnati said. "I am asking you, do those bandages that we have been using look similar to the ones that he had on his hands on April the 7th?"

"Similar, yes," Rita replied.

She testified about seeing Richard in Penney's on April 7 use a credit card to purchase tennis shoes, a pair of blue jeans, and a jean jacket. But when asked whether she had possession of the credit card, the tension grew.

"The first store clerk from J. C. Penney's testified that you got the credit card out of Richard Nitz's possession. Are you the woman, Mrs. Brookmyer, or is this some strange woman that just bopped in there into the store that night?"

"I don't know what woman or women may have bopped into the store, but I was there when Richard put the things on the counter for the cash register," Rita answered.

"Okay, you were the woman with Richard Nitz when he was using Michael Miley's credit cards on April the 7th at J. C. Penney's, correct?"

"I was with Richard when he purchased some things with a credit card on April the 7th, yes."

"All right," Garnati said. "You are the one who got the credit card from him so that it could be used, is that correct?"

"On April the 7th I don't believe so," Rita said.

During our visits, Rita told me a slightly different story. While confirming the April 8 trip with Richard to Paducah, she said that Betty

Boyer went with Richard to the Paducah mall on April 7. She said that Drew told her not to say anything about Betty going to Paducah on April 7. "He said that we didn't want to upset Betty and cause her to make up more stories." From the beginning of the trial, Rita did not believe that Betty would testify against her. And as for the April 8 trip to Paducah, Rita said that Richard stopped by the trailer that day and told her they needed to pick up Betty's children. It was not until they had reached Paducah that Rita realized they were going to the mall.

The prosecutor moved to the night of April 8, asking Rita about the credit cards and whether she willingly helped Richard.

"All right, you got the credit card from him at that first store on April 8, correct?"

"He told me to get the wallet out of his pocket," she said.

"And you did it, right?" Garnati asked.

"Yes, I did," she answered.

"And no threats made to you, right?" Garnati asked.

"Wrong, there were very many threats made to me," Rita answered.

"Okay, at the time that he told you to get the credit card out of his wallet, there was a threat made to you?" Garnati asked.

"There had been verbal threats all the way down there and menacing looks like if you don't do this you are going to be sorry," Rita said.

"Looks?" Garnati asked.

"Yes," Rita said. "Looks to accompany the threats that he had made verbally on the way down there."

"Okay, so he looked at you menacingly, is that correct?" Garnati asked.

"At that time, yes," Rita said.

Rita was asked whether she knew whose credit card was being used by Richard. "At the time on the 7th when he was using the card, I was not sure," Rita said. She saw the name Michael on the card and wondered whether Richard had obtained a credit card with her son's name, Charles Michael Haywood, on it. But on April 8 when she signed the card "Michael D. Miley," she knew it was not Richard's card. Still she never questioned him. For someone familiar with battered women, this behavior might seem logical, but for Garnati it was highly suspicious.

Garnati moved back to the evening of April 7, after Richard and Rita left the Paducah mall and their car broke down close to Johnson's house. Johnson had testified that Richard and Rita walked down the road holding hands, but Rita told Garnati that Richard was forcibly holding her wrist.

Garnati asked whether she was being forced to go with Richard to the Paducah mall on April 8, and when Rita answered yes, Garnati could not resist. "All right," he said. "Let me see, was he giving you these mean looks again?"

"No," Rita answered. "On April the 8th he had a knife to my throat."

When asked whether they stopped anywhere on the way to Paducah on April 8, Rita said Richard drove down a country road next to a field, a few miles from her trailer. After telling her to stay in the car, Richard walked to the middle of the field, bent over, and picked up a knife.

"Okay, you didn't tell the police about that on April 28 when you were interviewed at your trailer, did you?" Garnati asked.

"I am not sure if I mentioned it on April 28 when the officers were there or not," Rita said. "If I did, that would have been the first time that the police would have been told."

"Okay, if you did not say it on April 28, you did not bring it up any other time during this whole investigation, did you?" Garnati questioned.

"I brought it up to my attorneys," Rita answered. "In my opinion it was the attorneys' duty to contact the authorities."

"You had plenty of chances to talk to the authorities, didn't you?" Garnati asked.

"No," Rita said. "Not without an attorney there for representation."

"Okay, Richard Nitz was arrested on May the 6th, is that correct?" Garnati asked.

"I believe so, yes," Rita answered.

"All right, and on that day do you remember getting a visit from Sergeant Sylvester and Detective Burns?" Garnati asked.

"There were two officers," she said.

"And they asked you if you had information that could be helpful to the investigation, correct?" Garnati asked.

"What I remember them asking me is if I wanted to talk now," Rita said.

"All right, did you talk?" Garnati asked.

"I asked them if I could have an attorney present and they denied me," Rita said.

"What about the head of Michael Miley, Mrs. Brookmyer? Do you know where that's at?"

"Not specifically, no," Rita answered.

"Okay, do you have any information about it?" Garnati asked.

"The information that I gave you previously," Rita said.

"Okay, and how long did it take you to give us information about Michael Miley's head?" Garnati asked.

Garnati intended to show that Rita waited until August 11, 1989—more than a year after the death of Michael Miley—to give the authorities information about the location of Miley's head. Rita said that she made several attempts, while locked up in the Williamson County Jail, to speak with Garnati. She said that Richard told her the approximate location of the head in June of 1988, when the two were meeting with their attorneys, discussing a joint defense. This discussion occurred before the decision to have separate trials had been made.

Rita maintained that she told her attorneys about the information concerning the location of the head but did not know whether they had told the authorities. This statement did not satisfy Garnati.

"Isn't it true that if we had given you a deal and, you know, reduced or dropped these charges that you would have given us the information?" Garnati asked.

"I gave you the information regardless, sir," Rita said.

"On August the 11th, right?" Garnati asked.

"When I told you personally it was in August and if you had been notified previously I am not sure," Rita answered.

Garnati moved the questioning back to April 28, 1988, the day of the search warrant when Rita was questioned by three police officers. Rita was asked whether somebody by the name of Murphy admitted to her that he killed Michael Miley.

"No," Rita replied. "Glen Murphy had threatened me the week previously at my house."

"I want to get this straight, Miss Brookmyer. You did not tell the police that Glen Murphy admitted to you that he had killed a person and put them on forest property and done something to conceal his body?"

"He had said that previously he had," Rita said. "But he did not say it was Michael Miley."

"Okay, so Glen Murphy is admitting to some murder out there that we don't even know about, right?" Garnati asked.

"Whether he was admitting it or using that to frighten me, I'm not sure," Rita said. "It did frighten me."

At the end of Garnati's cross-examination, the judge asked Drew whether he had any redirect examination, and he answered, "No, your honor."

Each time I read through the trial transcript, I wondered why Rita was allowed to testify. What did Drew hope or expect to gain? Although little new information emerged, she might have been damaged. An air of uncooperativeness rose when Garnati focused on the fact that Rita waited more than one year to provide information about the location of Miley's head. And a combative nature surfaced as Garnati and Rita bickered back and forth throughout the questioning. If the jury favored a strong woman, one who stood up to Garnati and returned his volleys, then she won. But if the jury—a mixture of men and women living in the late 1980s in rural southern Illinois—favored a more passive woman, then she lost.

Fourteen years later Rita said that during the months leading to her trial, she sent several notes to Garnati, asking for a meeting. But each time, they were ignored. When I asked about the location of the head, she said that Richard and his friends did the same thing they had done with deer that were killed out of season. They buried Miley's head in a bag close to the water where the ground was soft.

I was surprised by her comment and asked, "Did Richard admit killing Michael Miley?"

"No," she answered. "He never told me that he killed Miley. He just said they, meaning he and his friends, buried the head. I don't know whether he killed Miley or if he was just there."

16 Separate the Wheat from the Chaff

It was September 21, 1989. Except for the occasional shuffling of papers, I imagine, the courtroom was quiet. Each attorney checked his notes, whispered to his assistant, and readied to perform as he had been trained to do. The jury waited. So much rested on the summations: each attorney had a last chance to spin his story in the most favorable way.

The closing arguments were intended to be balanced summaries of the facts presented by the state and the defense, allowing the clouds of doubt to disappear and a vision of truth to emerge. The jury, after hearing each side, would determine the guilt or innocence of Rita Nitz. It all seemed so simple, so predictable, as if fact and fiction could be pigeonholed into black and white. But after two years of searching, the truth was beyond my grasp.

Garnati began. "A person is legally responsible for the conduct of another person when either before or during the commission of an offense and with the intent to promote or facilitate the commission of that offense the person knowingly solicits, aids, abets, agrees to aid or attempts to aid that other person in the planning or commission of the offense." Plainly stated, if Rita, in any way, helped Richard Nitz kill Michael Miley, she was guilty of first-degree murder. The evidence, according to Garnati, showed that Rita watched Richard Nitz beat Michael Miley with a baseball bat and helped load the body into the trunk of Miley's car; and Rita assisted Richard by driving one of the cars to an isolated spot where Richard shot and decapitated Michael Miley.

This was a repeat performance for Garnati. Since Richard's trial had been conducted one year earlier, Garnati's speech was, possibly, smooth and steady and confident as he looked each jury member in the eye.

I could not help but wonder whether an observer had been fascinated by the way in which allegations, when spoken with certainty, unfolded as truth. Garnati declared that Richard's motive for murder was his habitual hatred for homosexual people and that Rita, Richard's loving and obedient wife, had been a willing partner. He listed a string of allegations to support the contention that Richard and Rita's dislike for the homosexual community was a matter of record.

There was the testimony of Charles Brookmyer that Rita was a co-leader of the Trog Club; there was the testimony of Betty Boyer that during the summer of 1987, Richard and Rita had come by her home and asked whether anyone wanted to go and harass some homosexuals; and there was Rita's posting of bond money for Richard after he had been charged with assaulting and intimidating homosexual men.

"Richard's behavior was obvious and Rita did nothing to stop it," Garnati said.

Garnati believed that Rita bought the gun that Richard used to shoot Michael Miley. Curt Ehlers, a Jackson County deputy sheriff, had testified that he saw Richard looking at handguns with a woman whom he could not identify but assumed to be Richard's wife.

But the heart of Garnati's case and the only eyewitness that tied Rita to Miley's murder was Betty Boyer. Take Boyer away, and you have nothing but an unconnected string of allegations. Garnati knew the importance of Boyer's testimony. "Either Betty Boyer is telling the truth or Rita Nitz is telling the truth," Garnati said. "And when you look at all of the evidence in this case, Betty Boyer is the one telling the truth."

Garnati was masterful in spinning a web of allegations that he hoped would snare Rita in an inescapable trap. He drew conclusions that to some appeared sound but, on closer examination, might be classified in Logic 101 as sweeping generalizations in which the conclusions drawn far exceeded the evidence. "I used only delicious ingredients, so this sauce must be delicious."

Betty Boyer testified that the altercation between Richard Nitz and Miley occurred between ten and ten thirty p.m. at the Nitz trailer on April 6. Robby Buttry and Edwin Pierson testified that they saw Miley around ten thirty p.m. on April 6 at the Crab Orchard Lake parking lot, just one mile from the Nitz trailer.

"That fits in with what Betty Boyer told you," Garnati said. "That corroborates what Betty Boyer told you."

Betty Boyer testified that Michael Miley followed Richard and Rita home and had an argument with Richard. Edwin Pierson testified that Miley did not like to be harassed and said that once, when a truck pulled into the parking lot and the driver shone his spotlight on everyone, Miley became upset and raced after the truck. Michael's father said that his son did not like to be called names and that although he was not a fighter, he would not back down from a verbal confrontation.

"That's another piece of corroboration," Garnati said.

Betty Boyer testified that Richard Nitz took a baseball bat from his Dodge Charger and attacked Michael Miley. "What did the police find on April 28, 1988?" Garnati asked. "They found a baseball bat in there." Boyer said that when Richard hit Miley several times in the head with a baseball bat, none of the blows struck below the neck. Furthermore, the pathologist, Dr. Tsai, reported that no marks or blows were found below the neck. Again, according to Garnati, this finding proved that Boyer was telling the truth.

Betty Boyer testified that Miley's head was partially caved in. "Rita Nitz corroborates that fact," Garnati said. "I'm telling you that because Rita does not want us to find the head. She has known where that head has been from the very beginning. She does not want us to find the head because she knows what we would find. We would find evidence of trauma with some type of baseball bat or blunt instrument, and we would probably find that there are two or three bullet holes in the head."

Garnati continued his summation by saying that Barbara Winkler testified about Rita's admission of guilt in the Williamson County Jail; Rita, and not Betty, went with Richard to the Paducah mall and used a dead man's credit cards; and finally, Betty testified that Richard and Rita loaded Miley's body into the trunk of Miley's car. This last statement was corroborated by the campers who found Miley's body in the trunk of his car. "Yes, ladies and gentlemen, Betty Boyer is telling the truth," Garnati said.

I was surprised when Rita told me that she had not been concerned about the impending verdict when Garnati wrapped up his closing remarks. "I was not worried," Rita said. "I knew there was no way they could find me guilty." How could she not taste the fear that worry breeds? I saw something quite different as I looked through Rita's eyes, past her skull, and into the gray matter. A place where two become one. A place where I saw the crisp chill of terror that occurs in one who believes hell will never end. A place Drew might have seen when he began his closing arguments on that warm day in September, some sixteen days after the trial had begun.

"I have this thing I call a cotton mouth," Drew said. "I have to take a small handful of pills every day, and I get a little dry. I have to do that to keep myself going, but in any event I would like to start off by telling you that I have never had a case that has impacted on me, that has bothered me and caused me to feel the responsibility that this case has. ... I have lost sleep, and as big as I am it is hard to tell, but I have lost about twenty pounds." Drew went on to describe the responsibility he felt and how the verdict would impact Rita for the rest of her life. "It plum scares me to death," Drew said.

The publicity that the case received worried Drew. Although the trial had been moved forty miles down the road, the name *Nitz* clung to Rita like a straitjacket. To be a Nitz carried the kiss of death, and to have married a Nitz was even more damaging. After all, how in the world could a person of character have married Richard Nitz? This was Drew's dilemma as he pleaded with the jury to move past the name.

Drew said that Boyer's testimony was laced with lies that built a wall of deception. Boyer testified that while babysitting at the Nitz trailer, she received a collect call from Richard on the evening that Michael Miley was killed; Betty testified that Chucky rode the school bus home on April 6. Both statements were proven wrong.

Boyer's memory about the location of the cars outside the trailer and where Richard and Rita went on the evening of April 6 changed from Richard's trial to Rita's trial. The inconsistencies were numerous. Boyer admitted that her eyesight was poor and that without glasses, things appeared fuzzy. This admission, plus her testimony that she witnessed the crime through a window in a lit room without any effort to block out the light, added to the claim that Boyer could not have seen Richard beating Miley with a baseball bat.

Boyer's story of Richard's attack at the trailer came after several days and several hours of interrogation by the police. Betty Boyer testified that before she told her story, she had been threatened with jail and the loss of her children. "She was psychologically raped," Drew said. Boyer was easily led by suggestion. Drew told the jury how he led her to say that Miley's head was caved in from the beating. "Only after my suggestion," Drew said, "did Betty describe the condition of the head."

Drew said that Boyer was arrested by a Williamson County officer on July 27, 1988, for knocking a child to the ground. She spent the night in jail but was miraculously released the next morning, one month before she would appear as the state's witness at Richard's trial. And while on the witness stand, Boyer admitted that she had asked for a written guarantee that she would not be prosecuted for the pending charge. Drew suggested foul play.

Drew found it unlikely that Miley, a man who was five feet six inches tall and weighed 120 pounds, followed Richard Nitz, a man who had a reputation for hating homosexuals, and verbally attack him. It does not make sense, Drew would say. And it seems impossible for Richard, in a fit of rage, to hit Miley numerous times with a baseball bat and not inflict glancing or direct blows anywhere below the head. It does not make sense.

No traces of blood, hair, or human tissue were found on the baseball bat, the knife, or the concrete patio where Boyer said that Miley fell. In fact, no physical evidence at all was found at the alleged crime scene. The bat was old and dull and lacked any protective finish. Any blood would have soaked into the porous wood and left a persistent stain—one that could not have been scrubbed away or diluted by an April rain.

Drew dismissed the idea of a Trog Club and Rita being called Trogette as one big joke on Richard. "Look at Richard's photo," Drew said. "The man looks like a cave man, a Troglodyte. It was just a joke."

Barbara Winkler, the prosecution's second big witness, is a "pitiful person," Drew said. "My heart goes out to her in a sense. I suspect she is borderline defective, maybe retarded." Winkler is nineteen, has two children, and has been in jail in at least two or three other states. After reaching a plea agreement, nine counts of forgery were dropped and Winkler pleaded guilty to a charge of theft. She will serve three years in prison. "I suggest to you that [Winkler's testimony] was purchased testimony," Drew said. "It was bought and paid for."

The burden of proof, as Drew explained, was on the state to show beyond a reasonable doubt that Rita Nitz murdered Michael Miley. Rita did not have to prove anything; she was not being charged with concealment of a homicide, Drew said. Rita was being charged with murder. There was no physical evidence to link Rita to the crime, and the state's only witness was Betty Boyer.

"I live across from the church up in Vienna," Drew said. "I have never set foot in it, but I want to tell you that I have asked the Lord to help you to separate the wheat from the chaff. The state's testimony and evidence [are] so fraught with fraud and deceit that this case cries out for justice."

Robert Drew finished and slid into his chair next to Rita. Charles Garnati walked toward the jury and began the prosecutorial rebuttal: another chance to erase any doubts the defense had raised. He came to the defense of Betty Boyer, the state's most valuable witness, and asked the jury not to be so hard on her. He believed it unfair to expect Boyer to remember dates and times and other numerical details eighteen months after the crime had been committed. He did not mention that Boyer had access to the transcript of her testimony at Richard's trial.

There was no evidence, according to Garnati, that Rita was afraid of Richard just prior to the murder. Although they had experienced problems in their marriage, Richard and Rita had patched things up and were spending time together. She went with Richard to the Paducah mall and used Michael Miley's credit cards. No one said Rita struggled to escape Richard's grip. That, he said, was a fact.

Rita was with Richard when shots were fired into the car of a gay man two nights before Miley's murder. "It is evidence, ladies and gentlemen," Garnati said. "Remember Bob Burns? He's the one who testified that they asked him about some statement they took from Richard, from a person named Richard Waide, and we checked that out, and we found out that these people, apparently Trog members, were out there with Richard and Rita Nitz two nights before, and that's the evidence." Drew objected, but the judge overruled. Two police reports said that Richard and two unidentified males were in a single car. The victim testified that no female had been involved.

Garnati referred to Rita's testimony when she claimed that Glen Murphy and his brother murdered Michael Miley and that they gave the credit cards to Richard for work he had done on their cars. "We found out that Murphy was in Florida on April the 6th. That's the way she is," Garnati said. "She can't tell the truth."

The jury was reminded that they did not have to believe that Rita shot Michael Miley. They just had to believe that Rita aided and abetted, that she helped him commit the murder. Garnati thanked the jury, turned, and walked to his chair. Quiet filled the room. Now the jury had to decide.

17 Citizens of Massac County

Rita was trapped in a web of despair that most people failed to understand. It was the kind of desperation that came from a confused mind, one whose wiring seemed slightly altered and never saw a different way. Any outbursts of laughter or hints of joy were unknowingly used to camouflage her sorrow. All her life, Rita had been riding a heat-seeking missile programed for hell.

Short of the death of your child or life in a vegetative state, nothing could be compared to the fear of spending your life in prison, where you are stripped of every freedom and reduced to a robot in human skin. At age thirty—a sweet spot in most lives—Rita was at the mercy of twelve fellow citizens who decided her hereafter. And who were they, these twelve residents of Massac County brought together to determine her guilt or innocence? Just ordinary citizens asked to perform a near God-like act. Only the insensitive did not feel the jury's burden to do the right thing, to show the public that they had answered the call, and to deal with the pressure from their peers. They sorted through sixteen days of information designed to convince rather than educate. After fifteen hundred pages of testimony and sixteen months of incarceration in the Williamson County Jail, it all came down to murder. The charges of robbery and a cover-up were dropped. The state wanted the home run; they wanted Rita for first-degree murder.

Judge Lowery read the instructions to the jury from a prepared script designed to avoid any future complaints about his procedure. Much of the testimony over the trial's sixteen days lacked clarity, but the directions, particularly for a criminal trial, had to be exact.

The defendant is presumed to be innocent of the charge against her. This presumption remains with her throughout every stage of the trial and during your deliberations on the verdict, and is not overcome unless from all the evidence in the case you are convinced beyond a reasonable doubt that the defendant is guilty.

The State has the burden of proving the guilt of the defendant beyond a reasonable doubt, and this burden remains on the State throughout the case. The defendant is not required to prove her innocence.

A person commits the offense of first degree murder when he kills an individual without lawful justification if, in performing the acts which cause the death, he intends to kill or do great bodily harm to that individual or another; *or* he knows that such acts will cause death to that individual or another; *or* he knows that such acts create a strong probability of death or great bodily harm to that individual or another.

A person is legally responsible for the conduct of another person when, either before or during the commission of an offense, and with the intent to promote or facilitate the commission of that offense, he knowingly solicits, aids, abets, agrees to aid or attempts to aid the other person in the planning or commission of the offense.

To sustain the charge of first degree murder, the State must prove the following propositions:

First: That the defendant or one for whose conduct she is legally responsible performed the acts which caused the death of Michael D. Miley.

and

Second: That when the defendant or one for whose conduct she is legally responsible did so, she intended to kill or do great bodily harm to Michael D. Miley; *or* she knew that his acts would cause death to Michael D. Miley; *or* she knew that his acts created a strong probability of death or great bodily harm to Michael D. Miley.

If you find from your consideration of all the evidence that each one of these propositions has been proved beyond a reasonable doubt, you should find the defendant guilty.

The instructions by Judge Lowery were meant to set straight any wrongs, to plow past any confusion, and to ensure that justice was served.

At ten forty-five a.m. on September 21, 1989, two bailiffs led the jury to a secluded room just down the hall from the courtroom. The room was simple: a long table, several chairs, and pads of yellow legal paper and pencils to record their thoughts. A coffeepot and a pitcher of water rested on an adjoining table. Just across the street and down the block from the courthouse was the Massac County Jail, the place where Rita waited.

At 4:25 p.m. on the same day, the attorneys were directed to the courtroom. The jury was not present. "The jury has requested the transcripts," Judge Lowery said. "I propose to answer that none are available. Do you have any objections to that, Mr. Drew?"

"No objection for the defense," Drew answered.

"I have no objection," Garnati said.

"Okay, thank you," Judge Lowery said.

At 6:20 p.m. the court was called back into session. The jury was out.

"The Court will come to order," Judge Lowery said. "Let me give you all a word of advice. I will tolerate no outburst from anyone, no commotion whatever. If anyone causes a disturbance they will go to jail. That's a promise. Don't try me. Bring the jury in."

At 6:25 p.m., silence was interrupted by the muffled rustle of twelve jury members returning to their chairs. Rita, Robert Drew, and Charles Garnati were present.

"Madam Foreman," the judge asked, "have you all reached a verdict?"

"Yes, Your Honor."

"Would you hand it to the bailiff, please? The Clerk will read the verdict."

"We, the jury, find the Defendant Rita J. Nitz guilty of the offense of First Degree Murder."

The verdict was swift and direct and to most, it would have buckled their knees. But the shock moved through Rita slowly and quietly like a morning tide. The jury got what it wanted: a lack of emotion that confirmed a just verdict. Still, Rita's statuelike stance was typical for someone accustomed to torment. Enough beatings and your body forgets how to flinch.

On October 15, 1989, when trees stood naked and birds could not hide from the morning sun, the half-filled courtroom waited for Judge Lowery's sentence. Nearly one month had passed since the jury found Rita guilty of first-degree murder, leaving everyone to wonder how long she would live in a six-by-nine-foot cell. Judge Lowery, dressed in his customary dark gown, sat God-like in a leather chair elevated above the rest of the people in the room. He had the power to inflict a sentence longer than life, one dampened with a touch of compassion, or one somewhere in between. He chose natural life without possibility of parole and justified his verdict by saying it was not as severe as the death sentence he had given to Richard Nitz one year earlier.

The reactions were expected: Miley's family believed the sentence was just, while Rita's family struggled to speak. Rita left the courtroom in shackles with a frozen face, an emotionless expression that caused some to mistakenly see it as an admission of guilt. Still, some fourteen years later, Rita's expression has not changed and her claims of innocence are rigid.

I felt like a detective as I searched for a secret that might piece together what happened on that spring night when Michael Miley was killed. Some people were reluctant to talk; some people had died; and many had moved away. Rita had recently signed a release that allowed me to look through her file at Larry Beard's law office. Although Beard was Rita's attorney only for the early months of her incarceration, still there was a six-inch stack of information to inspect.

I wiped off the dust-covered files and read through typed reports, memos, and even notes or fragmented thoughts scribbled across used napkins. In the midst of my hunt, a memo written by Robert Drew that described a conversation with Steven Gilbert grabbed my attention. That memo and a transcript of an interview between Steven and Kathy Gilbert and detectives J. R. Moore and J. J. Heischmidt of the Downstate Investigation Service were exhibits attached to a motion for a new trial that Drew filed on October 25, 1989. As I read the exhibits, another story began to unfold.

Part Three: **Truth**

18 In a Paper Sack next to the Water

Several days into Rita's trial, when things looked dire, Robert Drew received a telephone call from Steven Gilbert, a man Drew described as "lucid, and appeared to be very sincere and unemotional in his recitation of the facts that he knew." Steven said he had information that could change the outcome of Rita's trial. He insisted that he and his wife, Kathy, had overheard a conversation between Richard Waide (also known as Dickie Wade) and his mother, Mae Stout, in which the two talked about harassment of Michael Miley by Waide, Danny Walker, and Richard Nitz.

The transcript, dated September 6, 1989, of a recorded interview conducted by detectives J. R. Moore and J. J. Heischmidt of the Downstate Investigation Services with Steven and Kathy Gilbert, was a description of what happened at the home of Mae and Gary Stout, as seen and heard by Steven and Kathy Gilbert. Filed on October 25, 1989, the transcript was exhibit B attached to a motion for a new trial for Rita Nitz. The conversation that Mae Stout had with her son, Dickie Waide, had occurred between eleven and eleven thirty p.m. on or around April 10, 1988, one or two days after Michael Miley's body had been found.

Steven and Kathy Gilbert were visiting the Stouts, their friends for the previous thirteen years. The April evening was cool but warm enough for Gary Stout and Steven Gilbert to sit outside and drink a cold beer. According to the Gilberts, Dickie Waide stopped by not to pass the time of day but to establish an alibi. Waide seemed anxious. It was late at night, but for Dickie, tomorrow might have been too late.

"Mom, remember when I was down here?" asked Dickie Waide as he rattled off several dates."

"Yes, I remember. Why?" questioned Mae.

"Well, there is going to be some private detectives or investigators come talk to you about me being down here at this time," answered Waide. Mae looked confused. "Me and Danny Walker had been running around with this Richard Nitz, and we had been harassing faggots around Carbondale Park and different places. And one particular faggot came up dead." Waide identified the victim as Michael Miley, whose body was found in a car trunk at Rocky Comfort next to Progress Cemetery on April 9, 1988.

"It was real dark," said Kathy Gilbert, "and Dickie kept telling his mother, 'Now Mother, go look on the calendar because I was here and I know the dates.' He said the 6th, 7th, and 8th.... 'Now Dickie,' Mae said, 'I just can't do that,' but Dickie said, 'Mom, I've got to have an alibi that I was here the 6th, 7th, and 8th.'"

Waide told his mother that things got out of hand. Waide, Walker, and Richard Nitz were at a parking lot near Crab Orchard Lake when Nitz spotted Michael Miley, a man whom Nitz described as a faggot. They pulled up to his car and ordered him to step out. When Miley refused, Richard jumped from the passenger side of their car and ran toward Miley. Nitz pulled a gun from under his jacket and fired five times through the window. Waide added that Miley was unhurt and drove away.

According to the Gilberts, Dickie's story was inconsistent and, at the very least, questionable. They were puzzled that Richard Nitz, an ex-marine, could fire point-blank at Miley and not hit him. And they were puzzled when Waide told his mother about credit cards, a wallet, speakers, and some tapes that belonged to Miley. "Dickie said that he had traded Miley's stuff with someone and the stuff later ended up with the police," Kathy told the detectives. "How would Dickie have Miley's stuff if Miley was unhurt and drove away?" Kathy said that Dickie was visibly shaken and that Danny Walker had gone to Georgia for a couple of weeks. There was little doubt that something had happened.

Kathy was at Mae's house a few days later. "I was told a lot of things. 'Kathy, what do I do?' and I said, 'Well, Mae, I don't know. I'm not in your spot. I know that if I was, I'd want to protect him but nobody needs to protect someone if they did a bad crime.' 'Well,' Mae said to me, 'I know where the head is at.' That's exactly her words to me. 'I know where the head's at, exactly where the head's at.'"

"The head keeps sticking in my mind," Kathy told the detectives. "I know I heard her say where they put it. I don't know if the guy was beat to death, I don't know if he was shot, I haven't been keeping up on it, but I do know that she said the head was buried in a paper sack near water, right next to the water."

Steven questioned Betty Boyer's story about Miley following Richard Nitz home two or three days after Nitz allegedly shot five times into his car. If Nitz fired five times into Miley's car, why would Miley confront Nitz two or three days later? "It just doesn't make any sense to me," said Steven. "Now there's no way in the world I would follow a man home that just tried to blow me away."

When asked by the detectives if he ever heard whether Richard Nitz was bisexual or homosexual, Steven said, "I heard that Richard Nitz hated faggots and loved to whip on 'em. And Danny Walker hated them just as much." Steven had heard stories about how Walker used a bat on gay men.

Since the conversations between Dickie and Mae and between Mae and Kathy had taken place one year earlier, the detectives wondered why the Gilberts waited so long to report them. "Well," Steven said, "they had the man, that's just the way I looked at it. Dickie had told his story, and the police arrested Richard Nitz and charged him with murder. The next thing you know, they convicted him of it. Well, they did their job."

But now, when it looked as though Rita might spend the rest of her life in prison, the Gilberts felt uneasy. They did not believe that Rita had anything to do with Miley's death. "I've got a sneaking suspicion when Richard Nitz pulled the trigger that night, the man did not drive off," said Steven. "Danny or Dickie drove that car off. I'm positive of it, just the way Dickie's attitude was."

As I read through the transcript, I wondered about the credibility of the Gilberts, why the jury never heard their story, and what Rita thought when she heard about the conversation. I also wondered how men could talk about looking for faggots with the same emotional detachment they had from squirrel hunting or going to stir up a covey of quail.

I called Steven Gilbert and explained that I was writing a book about Rita Nitz and had come across a transcript of the Gilberts' September 6, 1989, interview. Gilbert was not excited or upset by my telephone call. But maybe that was because a call from the past, especially twelve years ago, delivered a mild shock. He was pleasant, helpful, and steadfast in his story. "I stand by every word in that report," Steven said. I saw no ulterior motive as to why the Gilberts told their story. After all, they had been friends with the Stouts for more than thirteen years and their revelations could have placed their friendship in jeopardy.

"No one knew about it for some nine years," was Steven's response when asked what the Stouts said when they found out he had called Robert Drew. Steven explained that after the interview with the detectives from the Downstate Investigation Service, he and his wife were told to be prepared to testify at Rita's trial. Later, when the Gilberts were called and told that they would not be asked to testify, Steven and Kathy decided to tell no one. Not until Richard's retrial in 1997 did the interview became known to the Stouts and Dickie Waide.

Maybe it was because so many years had passed that the Stouts were not openly upset with the Gilberts. "Dickie Waide was livid," said Steven. "He couldn't believe that we had called Robert Drew."

"Well, I guess your relationship with Waide is strained," I asked.

"No, it's okay," answered Steven. "Dickie Waide is our son-in-law."

"Your son-in-law?" I asked.

"Yes, four years ago, in 1997, they were married." Steven explained that at the time of the conversation on April 10, 1988, Dickie was twenty-three and their daughter was ten. Now Dickie was thirty-six and their daughter was twenty-three.

"Well, how do you feel about Dickie marrying your daughter?" I asked.

"I asked Dickie point-blank whether or not he had anything to do with the murder of Michael Miley," Steven said. "He said he did not. I have to believe that he wouldn't do such a thing."

"What about the prosecution?" I asked. "What did they say about your story?"

"They didn't say anything," Steven answered. "They never asked us a single question."

I do not know what surprised me the most: the alleged conversation on April 10, 1988, the fact that the prosecution never questioned the Gilberts, or the knowledge that Dickie Waide was the Gilberts' son-in-law.

After my telephone conversation with Steven Gilbert, I looked through the trial transcript and found no indication that the jury knew anything about the Gilberts' story. When I asked Rita about the Gilberts, she rolled her eyes in disgust.

"One morning," Rita said, "Drew came to the trial and said that someone called who had information that implicated other people in Miley's murder. I remember thanking God that someone has finally come forward with the truth. But the next day, Drew said it was nothing. The Gilberts weren't reliable, and as a result, they wouldn't be called."

Rita's January 26, 2002, letter to me exploded with flying fragments of verbal shrapnel: "You're a Garnati clone; you disappoint me; and I should have known better than to ever think you would be any different." A second letter was more of the same: "I am still undecided as to whether you are a complete numb-skull, or totally uncaring, or just blinded by your own ambitions and theories, or taking liberty with creative license to extreme measures."

Rita insisted a January 15 letter I had written contained a barrage of hurtful questions. But each time I read the letter, hoping to discover what she found so disturbing, I was confused. My questions to Rita were benign, or so I thought, and from the beginning of my search, I had vowed to never intentionally hurt Rita. That was my reality, but for the moment, that reality had been shattered.

I had reached a point in my investigation at which I was reading the part of the trial transcript that dealt with the search warrant. According to the transcript, Rita had made statements during the day of the search that were new to me. The times she talked about first seeing the credit cards, the comments made by Glen Murphy, and the gathering of Murphy, Waide, Walker, Boyer, Earlene, and Richard—all at her trailer—made me wonder whether she had been truthful with me.

I had so many questions, but unlike under normal circumstances, I could not pick up the phone and call her. Maybe I should have waited until I saw her at the Dwight Correctional Center, where I could have asked my questions, watched her body movements, and heard her response. But that would not have satisfied my need for answers. On January 15, 2002, I had made a list of four or five questions—all tactfully constructed, I thought—that addressed my concerns, and I sent the letter to Rita. After her curt reply, a six-month standoff began.

According to Rita's letters, I had violated her trust, and not unlike the rest of society, I had never believed her story. I suffered a certain amount of guilt as I wondered whether I had been less than open in my dealings with Rita, and while depressed, I sent her a letter of apology, expressing regret for anything that I said that caused her harm.

Two people whom I knew would be honest in their assessment read Rita's and my letters. Although they agreed that Rita was upset, they did not view my letters as offensive. But as I later discovered, some of Rita's fellow inmates thought differently: Rita had done nothing wrong, and I had a problem.

Hoping to solicit some input and to restore a line of communication with Rita, I sent a draft of my chapter that dealt with the search warrant. I assumed there would be some information in this chapter that Rita would challenge, and as so many times before, I gave her an opportunity to dispute what I had written. Still no response.

While making my weekly check of the prison Web site and clicking onto Rita's name, I was shocked by what I found: a photo of Rita with her hair cut to the scalp. She was someone I barely knew. Before prison, Rita's hair had brushed her waist, and for the past fourteen years, her thick, dark brown hair rested on her shoulders. Six months later my suspicions were confirmed. Rita said that cutting her hair was a form of self-mutilation and that I was the cause.

Rita had been open with me about her personal history, her past relationships, and her abusive background, but certain parts of her account of the murder were unclear. Perhaps she was not telling me everything, or her knowledge of the crime was limited, or I could not grasp the complexity of the crime.

Eventually I realized that some good had come from our break in communication. The distance allowed me greater objectivity, and although my compassion for Rita never wavered, my search for the truth was energized.

Weeks dragged into months, and Rita still refused to meet with me. Her occasional letter was addressed to "Mr. Lawrence Franklin," rather than "Larry." She was aloof. I sent another chapter, which I believed to be nonthreatening, one that Rita could appreciate. Still no response.

19 Photographs, Dope, and Queers

Today, some sixteen years after the trial, I am interested in how the jury sorted through days of testimony and separated fact from fiction and, after two years of research, why I still find truth and deception intertwined like a collage of dark colors. After all, we do not know how Michael Miley died, leaving the murder weapon in doubt; the alleged crime scene and baseball bat had no traces of blood or human tissue; and the state's only eyewitness, Betty Boyer, not only had bad eyesight but would have had trouble with single-digit multiplication tables.

Obtaining a transcript of the jury selection process was simple; locating the jury members was not so easy. Some had moved from the area, one had died, and others were just impossible to find. Still, I talked with four jurors, enough to glimpse into what happened in that jury room on September 21, 1989. Each person seemed sincere, honest, and while understanding the magnitude of their task, comfortable with his or her decision. This was no conspiracy. The jury was made up of twelve hard-working people looking to do the right thing.

At the beginning of deliberation, ten of the twelve jury members were confident of Rita's guilt, while two thought Rita had been forced to assist Richard in the murder of Michael Miley. In less than eight hours—between 10:45 a.m. and 6:25 p.m.—they had chosen a foreman, eaten two meals, and increased the guilty votes to twelve. For most, it was an easy decision.

Time had dampened some memories, while others held a freshness. One man said the trip to the Paducah mall convinced him that Rita was guilty; another cited Rita's testimony as proof; and one imaginative person said that Rita's body language told it all. "I could tell by the way she carried herself," he said. "There was no doubt in her guilt."

"If only the defense would have shown that Rita was forced to do what Richard wanted," one woman explained. "Then, I may have voted not guilty."

Another expressed her disgust: "Photographs of Miley's body, dope, and queers. It was all a big mess."

Since the charge against Rita was first-degree murder, the state needed to prove beyond a reasonable doubt that she aided or supported Richard in killing Michael Miley. The credit cards, alleged harassment, Rita's testimony, and body language were subordinate. The only eyewitness who tied Rita to the crime of murder was Betty Boyer, and since there was no physical evidence, we were left with Boyer's word. For me, guilt or innocence rested on Betty Boyer's testimony. But for the jury members I talked to, memories of Boyer disappeared somewhere in the shadows of a long-ago trial.

Rita never understood the jury's decision. I too wondered why they did not base their decision on Betty Boyer or at least remember her significance. Lately the riddle seems to have an answer. I read articles about jury psychology, hoping to understand how juries make decisions. Although what I found saddened me, it was understandable.

Nancy Pennington and Reid Hastie, psychologists at the University of Colorado, wrote "A Cognitive Theory of Juror Decision Making: The Story Model," published in 1991 in the *Cardoza Law Review*, explaining how juries arrive at their decisions. Pennington and Hastie recruited people called for jury duty but not impaneled to serve for an actual trial. Instead, panels of recruits watched a movie of a murder trial reenacted by professional actors. The psychologists performed detailed interviews with each quasi juror, looking to find the reasoning that led them to an innocent or guilty verdict. They discovered that nearly half of what the jurors used as the basis for their decision had not been presented in the courtroom and came instead from each juror's life experiences, assumptions about human nature, and judgments about the character and psychology of the participants in the case.

Pennington and Hastie concluded that the jurors had paid attention to what was presented—collectively, the jury panels accurately recalled 93 percent of the facts in the case—but had found the testimony and evidence inadequate to make sense of what had occurred. They were spinning threads to connect the patches of evidence into a plausible plot that suited their experience. The jurors, in effect, were writing stories instead of analyzing details.

The essence of a trial, according to Dana K. Cole, a professor at the University of Akron School of Law, is storytelling—"telling a simple story passionately and succinctly." In "Psychodrama and the Training of Trial Lawyers: Finding the Story," Cole says the trial lawyer should present a case in a way that reveals not only what happened and why it happened but how it was experienced. Only then can the juror relate on an emotional level and become fully engaged.

The Synchronics Group, established in 1981 to assist attorneys with jury presentations, believes that jurors vote their hearts, their feelings, and their emotions and then find a legal hook to hang their decision on. Unless the jury is presented with a compelling story from the beginning, they will fill in the gaps with their imaginations and make a decision based on only a part of the evidence. Compelling stories, as the Synchronics Group points out, are not about facts but rather about higher themes of justice versus injustice, right versus wrong, truth versus lies, the good guy versus the bad guy, what is fair versus what is unfair. The decisions of juries are all about feelings: helping people they like, punishing people they do not like, righting a wrong, acting justly, acting fairly, and supporting institutions they believe in. The challenge is to tell a story that allows the jurors to feel good about voting for you.

During Rita's trial, the state told a story. Rita was a coleader of the Trog Club, a partner in crime, and the devoted wife of Richard Nitz. Together the couple rode their motorcycles across the countryside, drinking, doing drugs, and harassing gay men. Rita was a lowlife and someone easy to hate.

The defense was built on the expectation that no one would believe Betty Boyer, and as a result, Drew concentrated on explaining the inconsistencies in Boyer's testimony. He neglected to explain how Rita had an abusive childhood, was a battered woman, and according to all accounts, had a tremendous fear of Richard. No expert witnesses explained that battered women find it nearly impossible to escape the grasp of their batterer and that, like Miley, Rita was a victim as well. They never talked about Rita, a poor white woman who lived in a run-down trailer, struggled to make a better life for herself, and maintained a nearly straight-A average at John A. Logan College. The jury never heard about Rita, the fifteen-year-old girl saddled with an unplanned pregnancy, who chose to raise her child in an unwanted marriage rather than submit to an abortion. The jury never heard her story.

For the jury system to work properly, the prosecution and the defense must be equal. And that requires the attorneys and staff of both sides to have similar abilities, motivation, and funds to construct a compelling case. The jury members I interviewed agreed that disparities between the preparedness of the attorneys existed, even to the point of wondering whether the verdict might have been different if the attorneys had been reversed. They described Garnati as aggressive, well-prepared, and focused, while Drew seemed passive, shaky, and uninspired. I too can only conclude that if Garnati had been Rita's attorney, she would not be in prison today.

20 "Some like to eat, I like to fight"

Two juries believed that Richard Nitz murdered Michael Miley. He had spent a major part of his life in prison, he had a reputation for harassing gay men, and he had possession of Miley's credit cards. He was a likely suspect. Still, I had never seen any forensic evidence that tied Richard to the murder of Michael Miley, and I felt obliged to hear his story.

In late October 2002, I called the Menard Correctional Center for Richard's prison identification number and mailing address. Only Richard could add my name to his list of approved visitors. In a letter to him, I introduced myself as a journalist who was writing Rita's story and wanting to hear his side as well. (I assumed he would talk. After all, I was giving him the opportunity to tell his story and to refute Rita's claim.) But two weeks later, no response.

My second attempt was followed by a letter laced with contrasting themes. Richard said that I had been "snowballed" with Rita's stories of abuse and that if I chose to print her "fabricated claims," I would "meet head on with legal problems." And yet his charges were followed by an offer to place me on his visiting list. In a second letter, written in late December, he said I was on his visitation list and that we could discuss a fee for his input.

On New Year's Day 2003, I drove to the Menard Correctional Center, the state's second-oldest prison and largest maximum-security facility, where Richard had spent the previous fourteen years. Menard, as it is commonly called, was built in 1878 to house 1,460 prisoners, but the population had grown to 3,155. The building wrapped around a bluff next to Chester, Illinois, on the east, while the Mississippi River claimed its western border. All vegetation was gone, and a light rain fell from a low, gray sky. The view seemed to be a black-and-white photo stuck in time. And its darkness suggested that blood, sweat, and male urine had leaked through the prison walls.

Any anxiety I held surfaced when I pulled into the parking lot and watched a security van rush my way, blocking any possibility of escape. Two male officers climbed from their car and asked whether I was a visitor. When I answered yes, they searched me, looked through my car, and asked me to open the trunk. Minutes later, they pointed me toward the check-in building, a small brick structure some two hundred yards south. After a second search, I moved to a waiting room, where visitors stayed while inmates were brought to the visit room.

The waiting room, with its wooden floors and plastered walls, was furnished with dark wooden chairs and two sofas covered in cracked red vinyl. High ceilings added to the gymlike acoustics that held sounds in the air like a morning fog. Metal doors slammed shut, guards talked in booming tones, and flushing stools were heard throughout the prison wing. I sat alone, thinking of Richard and waiting for his name to be announced through a speaker on the wall. I was eager to meet him, a man whose crime was frequently discussed in southern Illinois coffee shops, a man described in extremes. Rita said that while he could be sweet and kind, he could quickly turn; Larry Beard said that although Richard once had run down a thief and held him until the police arrived, he loved to fight; and Richard's first wife, Jean Nitz, said that although their marriage had ended in divorce, he was a caring man.

It had been nearly two years since I called Jean Nitz and told her that I was writing a book about Rita Nitz and was looking into Richard's background. Jean told me they met when she was a church volunteer who visited inmates at the Menard prison, and according to her, they fell in love and were married when he was released from prison. At the time, Jean was fifty; Richard was twenty-eight.

"He was a gentle man and never laid a hand on me."

As she reminisced, she talked about her severe back pain that, even with medication, kept her awake at night. "He couldn't stand to see me in pain," she said. "One night I cried. It hurt so much. Richard went outside and jacked the car up and let the frame fall on his hand. Then he went to the emergency room with a crushed and bloodied hand and brought me the pain medication they gave him."

I was stunned. "He let the car frame drop on his hand?" I asked.

"Yes he did," Jean said. "You should go meet him."

Now, as I sat in the waiting room, a couple who appeared to be in their early sixties said they were here to see their son. "He's our baby," the lady said. Two middle-aged women and a man from Georgia joined us. One by one, names of inmates were announced through the speaker. *Visitor for Richard Nitz. Visitor for Richard Nitz.*

I stood and walked to an officer who stood behind a row of metal bars. He unlatched the door, took my name, and opened a second set of doors leading to a stairwell that stretched to the second floor. To the left was the visit room. In the front of the room, Richard sat at one of several round tables with metal seats welded to their sides. The room was long and rectangular, with high ceilings, a row of vending machines at the rear, and a desk with several guards at the front. Richard, dressed in dark blue pants and a light blue long-sleeved shirt open at the collar, sat stiltedly and stared into nothingness.

I approached his table and spoke. "Richard?"

We both leaned across the table and shook with a firm but cautious grip. I kept a vacant seat between us. Except for a missing front tooth, he looked like his prison photo on the Illinois Department of Corrections Web site: dark brown hair that reached the bottom of his neck, deep green eyes, and a broad nose, possibly flattened by blows to his face.

"Well," I said, "it's good to meet you." He nodded slightly. "I guess I should begin by telling you why I'm writing about Rita."

His response was muffled. I stood and sat next to him. "Now we can hear better," I said. I explained that when I wrote an essay about hate crimes, I was drawn to the Miley murder, which had been publicized as such an extreme crime, and shocked by Rita's life sentence. Then I talked about her trial transcript and that I believed the state had failed to prove her guilty beyond a reasonable doubt. As I talked, he saw that I had done my homework and was familiar with the case and he seemed to accept my presence.

"Boyer's testimony was ridiculous," he said disgustedly in his baritone voice. "I don't know why they believed her."

I nodded.

"When I get another trial," Richard said, "there's no way I'll lose."

"Why do you say that?" I asked.

At his most recent trial, his second, he said four jury members did not believe that he had committed the crime. But pressure from other jury members made them change their minds. Next time would be different, he said.

"Do you think you'll get another trial?" I asked.

He nodded. "Yes. I get up each day expecting to hear that I'm getting a new trial." I was surprised by his confidence.

I asked whether the state was paying his legal fees and, when he said no, asked how he could afford a Chicago attorney. "I can't," he said. "After my last trial, my attorney came to me and said that she wouldn't charge me. She believes that I'm innocent and said she will stick with me till this is over."

"Well, that's great for you," I said, surprised. Her confidence, if I was to believe Richard, suggested a measure of innocence.

"She said you can call her anytime," he said. "She'll talk about the case with you."

Weeks later, I called Aviva Futorian, Richard's attorney, and asked whether she was representing Richard for no fee. She answered yes. And when I asked if she was doing this because she believed that Richard was innocent or because the state failed to prove their case, Futorian answered yes to both questions. Her response cluttered my thoughts with more doubts, making me wonder whether Richard's bad reputation had brought him down.

The conversation with Richard was moving well, but I knew I had to ask the tough questions. "Did you have anything to do with the murder of Michael Miley?" I asked.

His eyes were steady. "No, I did not."

While I was not surprised by his answer, I looked for a clue, a hint of guilt. "Do you know who killed Miley?" I asked.

"Yes," he said. "It was Danny Walker and Dickie Waide."

"Do you have any proof?" I asked.

"No," he answered. "But I know it was them." He moved closer and raised his voice. "Are you with the FBI? Are you a policeman?"

I felt totally unprepared for his question, searching for a proper response. "What are you talking about?" I asked. "You wonder if I'm with the FBI?"

He studied my face. "Yes," he answered. "Are you with the police?"

"Well, I can assure you that I'm not a law enforcement officer of any kind. I'm surprised you would ask that. I don't know what I can say to convince you."

"I got you on that one," he said as a smile returned to his face.

"Yes, you did." There was a pause, followed by our laughter, followed by another pause. "What about the credit cards?" I asked. "How did you end up with the credit cards?"

"Danny Walker and Betty Boyer gave them to me and Rita."

"Rita?" I questioned. "I've never heard that before." He chuckled, seemingly amused that he gave me information I did not know. "I heard that Walker gave you the credit cards for some work done on his transmission."

"Walker owed me money and Boyer owed Rita money," he said. "They asked us if we would take the cards for partial payment. I knew they were hot, but not that hot. It was a stupid mistake on my part."

"Well, if that was true," I said, "then Boyer might have had something to do with the murder."

"She probably did," he said.

"I've never heard this theory before," I said. Richard smiled slightly.

"Why do you hate Rita?" I asked.

Quickly he answered. "It's her fault that I'm in prison."

His remark was unexpected. "Why do you say that?" I asked.

"She took my attorney. Before her trial, she asked me who would be the best attorney and I told her about Paul Christenson. Then she went and got him for her postconviction work so I couldn't use him. Paul was a good trial attorney. He never lost to Garnati."

"Well, Christenson never did anything for her. I'm surprised that's why you hate her."

"Oh, that's not the only reason." He hesitated and continued. "She lies a lot."

"Are you talking about the abuse?" I asked. "Rita said that you abused her and she got a restraining order against you."

Clearly he was agitated again. "None of that crap happened," he bellowed. "She's made it all up." He leaned closer to me. "You really messed up when you took her for your main subject."

"Why do you say that?" I asked.

"Because she lies all the time," he complained.

I was taken by how easily he moved between good feelings that grew to laughter, to agitated ones that caused me to back off. The visiting room had filled. Occasionally an inmate passed our table and dropped a "Hey, how's it goin', Richard?" and Richard threw back a "Fine, man."

Richard agreed when I suggested that Rita's life sentence was extreme. "That's so ridiculous," he said. "She didn't have anything to do with any of this. She shouldn't be in prison."

"I've heard a lot of interesting stories about you," I said. "I've heard that you can be the nicest person in the world, fun to be with. And then I've heard that you really like to fight." I leaned back, waiting for his response.

A wide smile grew across his face. "Oh, I really liked to fight," he said. "And I still like to fight." His voice sparkled.

"Why do you like to fight so much?" I asked.

Richard thought for a moment and then spoke deliberately. "Some people like to eat, I like to fight." Now we were both laughing.

"Well, isn't there the danger that if you fight too much, you might cross the line? You might kill someone?"

Again, he thought before speaking. "When you eat, you eat until you're full. When I fight, I fight until I'm full. Then I stop." Our laughter continued. He quickly changed the subject. "What about some money?" he asked. "We haven't talked about the money."

"I can't pay you anything," I answered. "I'm not making any money, and I don't have any arrangement with Rita."

He moved closer and pointed his finger. "I don't care what arrangement you have with her. I'm talking about us."

"I can promise to tell your story," I said.

He hesitated and leaned closer and looked more direct. "I can't imagine that you'd spend all of this time working on a book without a bunch of money. It doesn't make sense."

"Well, this may be hard to understand," I said. "I'm doing this because I love to write. And now I find myself so interested in this story that it has become an obsession." I sounded more and more determined as I spoke. "Now I can't stop. I have to finish it."

Another wide smile, like the one before, spread across his face. He leaned forward, and his voice rose. "Do you like to fight?" We broke into laughter. At that moment I knew that he had made the connection. He loved to fight; I loved to write. We both had a passion.

Maybe we should have had a photo of Miley's headless body resting on our table. Then I would not have enjoyed myself so much.

Richard seemed to accept that I would not pay money for words but would tell his story. Our conversation continued. "Let's talk about theories," I said. "I obviously don't know how the murder occurred. So I'm left with different theories. You said that Walker and Waide committed the murder." He nodded. "Well, one theory is that it was Walker and Waide and you."

"What are you talking about?" he hollered. "You're throwing me in with the two of them."

I raised both hands off the table with the palms facing him. "Now we're just talking theories," I said. "You have to admit that this is one possible theory."

He calmed. "Well," he said, "that's not what happened."

I paused. "Maybe we should have a drink," I said. "I've got a debit card. Would you like a Coke or something to eat?"

"Sure," he said. "A Coke sounds good."

We walked to the vending machines, and I slid my card in and pulled out two Cokes. When I asked whether he wanted something to eat, he answered no. He said that he was trying to watch his weight. At five feet nine inches and 160 pounds and with a soldier's posture, he was obviously in good shape. We returned to our table and sat down.

I asked if he was familiar with the Gilbert interview. He answered yes but not until the time of Rita's trial, which was one year after his. During his second trial, he wanted the information to be made available to the jury, but the judge would not allow it. "If the jury had had that information," he said, "I wouldn't be sitting here."

"I was surprised that it wasn't used in Rita's trial," I said.

"Yes," he answered. "Her attorney dropped the ball on that one."

"What about Walker and Waide?" I asked. If they committed the murder and you're sitting in prison, you must be pissed off."

Richard said something about bastards and sons of bitches. "When I get out, I'll be paying them a visit."

"What will you do?" I asked.

"I'll inflict some pain," he answered with a determined look.

"Would you kill them?" I asked.

"No, I wouldn't kill them," he answered. "I'd just inflict a whole lot of pain so they'd know how much I'd suffered over the past years."

I asked him how old he was and how much of his life had been spent behind bars. He said he was fifty and, after a few seconds of thought, that he had spent twenty years in prison. The harsh reality seemed to bother him.

"What about this place?" I asked. "Is it scary?"

"Oh, it's not that bad," he answered. "They don't bother me that much. I have a reputation."

"A reputation?" I asked.

"Anyone who bothers me pays the price," he said.

"Some of these guys are huge," I said. "They look like they could be quite a handful."

"Size doesn't mean a thing," he said as he repeatedly tapped his finger to the side of his head. "It's all a mind set. I don't think about their size. I just do what has to be done."

"I talked with Mike Wright," I said, wanting to change the direction of our conversation. "I guess the two of you were good friends."

Richard smiled. "That's right. He was my best friend."

"I talked with Paul Hyler," I said. "Paul and Mike both agreed that Rita pushed your hot buttons."

"That's right," he said. "She had a way of doing that."

"Where were you on the night of the murder?" I asked.

"Oh, I don't know," he answered. "That was a long time ago." The tone of his voice demanded another question, suggesting that this was unimportant.

"What about Earlene Young?" I asked. "I often wonder what she knew about the murder."

"Earlene and Betty were good friends," he said. "I always believed that Earlene knew what happened and knew that Betty lied. She felt bad about it." He went on to say that when he was in jail, he received some money anonymously and suspected that it was from Earlene. "I think she felt bad about the truth not coming out and was going to talk. I think Betty killed her." Earlene's death, which occurred several months after Rita's trial, was due to an overdose of prescription drugs. But one of her brothers-in-law told me later the death was suspicious.

"I've never heard that before," I said. "Do you have any proof?" I asked.

"No," he answered. "I just believe that's what happened. Betty was afraid that Earlene was going to tell the truth."

I asked Richard about his paintings. He was noticeably pleased that I recognized his artistic side, but he downplayed his talents. Although his love for painting was strong, the cost and difficulty of obtaining supplies limited his affair. Some time later, I found photos of two of his paintings on an outdated Web site sponsored by the Illinois Coalition Against the Death Penalty. One showed a small boy being led by an older woman over a log laid across and above a small, swift stream. A larger-than-life guardian angel watched from above.

A guard walked to our table and said that I had ten minutes left for my visit. When I looked at my watch, I realized that we had talked for more than two hours. I asked Richard whether I could visit him again, and he said yes. We rose from our chairs, walked toward the exit, stopped, and shook hands. I said that I would see him again.

I left the room and made my way back to the check-in building, where I opened my locker and collected my things. It had been a good visit, covering a spectrum of emotions from the serious to the humorous, veiled in an air of sadness that left me drained and at the same time invigorated. Thoughts of my visit stayed with me for days, much like the lingering prison odors that hung deep in my nasal passages. At first I thought the odor was a mixture of smoke and the mold of Menard, but when I periodically checked my clothes for the origin of this pungent smell, I was baffled.

It was only later, during a conversation I had with Lisa, a writer friend, whom I had called to go over my interview with Richard, that I learned the origins of that odor. Toward the end of our discussion, I said I had a lingering smell that seemingly had been jammed up my nose, and I could not pinpoint its composition.

"I thought it was a mixture of smoke and mold," I said. "But now I think that it's something different."

"I know the smell," she said with an air of excitement. "I've experienced the same odor when I visited my male friend who is in a Nebraska prison."

"What do you think it is?" I asked.

"I think it's a male hormonal thing," she said.

"Meaning what?" I asked.

"Maybe it's a bit of smoke and mold mixed with male sweat, urine, and body fluids."

I paused and considered her explanation. "I think you might be right," I said. *Why should I be surprised?* I thought. *After two and a half years, the unexpected had become the expected.*

21 A Secret Map

On June 5, 2002, six months since Rita and I had last talked, I received a letter from her saying that if I was still interested, she would see me. Time had worn down my hopes of visiting her again, leaving me with a belief that I would finish the story without her help. Still I craved her input. My shoulders lifted slightly, and my breathing was freer than before. The months had moved slowly, but for whatever reason, Rita was ready to see me and I was grateful.

On June 14, two seasons past my last visit, when the ground was covered with snow, I drove into the parking lot at the Dwight Correctional Center. Minutes later, I sat with Rita at a small, round table in the visit room, where vending machines hugged the walls and intakes mopped the floor. We chose our words carefully. For the first time, I understood how my prodding was seen as an attack and Rita understood my need for questions. Although no new information surfaced, the line of communication had been restored. It was a new beginning.

One month later, we had an easy four-hour visit. Near the end of our conversation, as the clock approached one thirty p.m., Rita gave me the telephone number of a former inmate at Dwight whom I'll call

"Maggie"; I had attempted to contact her one year earlier when I sought information about women's prisons. We had never met, but her name was familiar.

When I returned home that night, I called Maggie and she talked with a friendly flair to her voice. She told me that Rita was one of her best friends and had watched her back while she was at the Dwight Correctional Center. "You can't imagine how bad that place is," Maggie said. "You've only seen the visit room. On the other side of the wall is hell. I told Rita that I would talk with you but that I wouldn't lie for her."

I was surprised by Maggie's frankness. "What do you know about the murder?" I asked.

"Oh, I know how it happened," Maggie answered. Her voice took on an air of excitement. "Rita told me everything." *This was so easy*, I thought. *I had been knocking my head against a wall for two and a half years and now I'd found someone with answers.*

"Tell me how it happened," I said.

"Well," Maggie said as she seemed to burst with information, "Richard was driving through the Grassy Bottoms, and a car was following him. When Richard stopped, the other car stopped. It was Michael Miley. It's such a shame. I used to work with Michael at a local restaurant. He was such a nice young man. Anyway, Miley got out of his car and walked up to Richard's. I don't know what was said, but Richard took a gun and shot him in the head."

I quickly thought of Walker's testimony at Richard's trial. Both stories were the same. "What happened next?" I asked.

"Richard put the body in Miley's car and drove to Rita's. He told Rita to get in the car, he wanted her to do something. Then Richard went to the garage and got one of those big machetes and got in the car. He drove to the spot where Miley's car was parked and told Rita to follow him. They went someplace in the Grassy Bottoms and stopped. Richard opened the trunk of Miley's car and pulled the dead body out and decapitated him in front of Rita. It really messed her up. Rita used to wake up screaming from nightmares when she was in the Williamson County Jail."

"Why didn't she tell the police?" I asked. *If Rita had told her story*, I thought, *she would be free today.*

"She was afraid to," Maggie answered. "Rita had gone to the Paducah mall with Richard when he used the credit cards. She was afraid they wouldn't believe her and she didn't want to go to jail."

"You seem to know a lot about this case," I said. "Did you know that Richard may have been bisexual?"

"Oh, yes, I know that," Maggie said. "And so was Rita."

"How do you know that?" I asked. *I couldn't imagine that I'd never heard this before. How could I have missed this?* I thought. *And Maggie was saying it in such a matter-of-fact way.*

"When Rita got a restraining order against Richard, she asked a woman to move in with her," Maggie said. "That just drove Richard over the edge."

"How could that be?" I asked as I struggled to understand. "The only woman staying with Rita at that time was Betty Boyer."

"That's right," Maggie said. "Betty and Rita were lovers."

"Are you sure?" I asked.

"I'm positive," Maggie answered.

I don't know why I ended our conversation. Maybe it was too much information for me to process or maybe it was the shock of it all or maybe I just needed time to think. "When can we get together and talk?" I asked. "You could be a big help to me."

We arranged to meet a few days later for breakfast. The days passed slowly, and I wondered whether this was Rita's way of telling me what happened on April 6, 1988. But when the day arrived, Maggie never appeared. I called and was told that she was not feeling well and I should check back later. Each time there was another excuse. Finally, after reaching Maggie, we rehashed her story. It was the same as before.

"Maybe we can get together on Tuesday after work," Maggie said. "I think I'll get off around one p.m. Maybe we can go get the head. The family needs to get that head back."

The shock was quick, yet certain. From getting together after work to finding the head, her voice had the same bouncy unattached sound. I hid my emotions while forcing myself to continue. "Tell me more."

"Well, I have a map of where the head is located," Maggie said. "Rita drew it for me when I was in prison. I got it out last night and looks like it wouldn't be that hard to find."

"How long have you had this map?" I asked.

"Oh, I don't know," Maggie said. "I guess for quite a while."

"Why haven't you told anyone?" My emotions were beginning to surface. "This is not right. The family has to know about this."

Maggie seemed surprised by my response. "Well, I don't know."

She hesitated. "If a friend tells you not to say anything, you don't say anything."

"I understand," I said while trying to calm myself. "Let's meet tomorrow, Tuesday at one p.m."

"Okay," Maggie answered. "I'll call you as soon as I get off work. Then we can meet."

Seconds later, I called the police officer I knew and asked for his advice. After we discussed my conversation with Maggie, he assured me, with a "don't worry about it" sound to his voice, that looking for a head was not illegal. But if I did find something, I was to notify the police immediately.

On Tuesday morning, I went to the office and tried to do some work, but my thoughts were elsewhere. One o'clock arrived but no telephone call. Two, three, and finally four o'clock passed, and still no call. At five, I called Maggie. She told me that she had car problems and hadn't been able to make it. Her voice was tense, so I asked whether there was a problem. She told me that she was having an argument with one of her kids and would have to call me back. I hung up and never heard from her again.

I decided to tell Rita what Maggie had said. I wanted to see her facial expression and body language in reaction to what I had to say. Two weeks later Rita and I sat in the visit room. After some small talk, I brought up my discussion with Maggie. I hoped that Rita would confirm what Maggie had told me and I would have my story, but Rita denied everything, from her prison confession to having witnessed the decapitation to a mysterious map showing the location of Miley's head. Rita couldn't imagine why or how Maggie had come up with such a story. For the most part, Rita appeared calm, yet small signs of anger surfaced when I told her that Maggie said she and Betty were lovers. I asked questions every imaginable way and still received the same answer: Rita was not with Richard when the murder or decapitation took place.

Later I compared Maggie's story with others I had been told. When Betty Boyer moved in with Rita, Roy Dulaney stayed at the trailer during the evening and Rita's cousin stayed during the daytime. Roy Dulaney said that he and Betty were having a romantic relationship while he was staying at the trailer. Roy was sleeping with Betty. If Maggie's allegations about Rita and Betty being lovers were false, what about the rest of her story?

And then there's the possibility that Rita had seen something so horrific that the event was blocked or buried in the deepest part of her brain, never to be recovered again. If Rita had seen what Maggie claimed—the decapitation of Michael Miley—it was logical to believe that Rita could not remember. Two psychologists, with whom I have shared parts of the story, suggested that Rita could have suppressed the memories of such events, and if that were true, I should push lightly or else something might surface that Rita could not handle without professional help.

22 "Do we have a problem?"

On Thursday, November 7, 2002, I pulled into the Phillips truck stop, just two miles east of the Dwight Correctional Center. The truck stop looked the same: a white wood-framed building where on-the-road truckers sat at a crowded counter. In a connecting room, a group of local men held one table and several women circled another. Quiet couples claimed three or four booths. I eased into a red vinyl booth and, like many times before, put away the truckers special—two eggs, bacon, hash browns, toast, and loads of black coffee. This place had become my sanctuary, where I reviewed my thoughts before driving to the prison.

A cold front had unzipped the clouds and lay open the blue sky, and the prison's frost-covered parking lot was more crowded than before. I arrived at the check-in room, and after twenty-five visits, I still relished each meeting. An attorney stood in front of me and completed his paperwork while the correctional officer called to have an inmate brought to the visit room. After stepping forward and saying hello to Officer Creek, I told her how much I liked her haircut. She ignored my remark and slid the sign-up sheet my way. Several people, maybe ten or so, had entered the room. Creek picked up the telephone. "Bring Rita Nitz down. She's got a visitor."

From the back of the line, someone yelled out, "Who's here to see Rita Nitz?"

I turned and looked his way. He stood about five feet ten inches and had dark hair combed back on the sides and time edged into his face, particularly at the corners of his eyes. His slim-cut jeans accented a rail-thin build, and his boots were pointed at the toes. We exchanged questioning looks.

"Okay," Creek bellowed. "Do we have a problem here?"

The man and I stared at each other, and then he asked if I was a writer. Quietly and firmly I answered yes. Everyone looked our way.

"Let's get something straight," Creek said. "I'm not going to have the two of you fighting when you go to the visit room."

"Oh, there's no problem," the man stated. "I know Larry. We can sit at the same table with Rita."

I remembered receiving a telephone call more than a year earlier from John Young, a friend of Rita's. After failing to reach me herself, Rita asked John to call me when she had been placed in segregation. She later told me that John was jealous and had a short fuse. For two years, she had had him removed from her visitation list. Yes, this was John Young.

"No," I answered. *My visit would be wasted if I didn't speak privately with Rita*, I thought. *And what about her letter filled with hints of suicide and how someone had threatened her?* "I need thirty minutes with her."

Creek's frustration grew. "Okay," she added. "This is how we're going to do it. Larry was first, so he gets to see Rita for three hours. Then he comes out and John can go in for three hours."

John's words quickened. "I just drove three hundred miles to see Rita, and I can't wait three hours. Come on, Larry," he said with disgust. "We can sit together."

"No. Give me thirty minutes. Then I'll leave." Believing that Rita would support me, I turned to Creek. "Why don't we let Rita decide?"

"Okay," Creek said. "Larry will go in first. I'll go in and ask Rita what she wants to do. Then I'll come out and tell John how we're going to handle this."

After being searched, I walked down the hallway leading to the visit room where Rita waited. I gave her a friendly hug. Rita said that she was surprised to see me and had not received the letter I had sent a week earlier telling her that I would be there on this day. As we sat at one of the round tables, I told her we had a problem, that John Young was here. Rita sighed and shook her head. "This is my shopping day, and now both of you are here," Rita said.

"What do you mean, your shopping day?" I asked. *How could anyone in prison have a shopping day?* I thought. *And what about my safety?*

"This is my commissary day," Rita snapped. "Do you think that we can go anytime we want? This is prison. I'm scheduled to go shopping at one p.m."

Her frown changed to laughter. This was the first time in nearly three years that I had seen her laugh. There were times when she saw a familiar inmate and a lighter side appeared, but I believed that was her outer shell—the side with the shield—and I was touching her inner self. "I told John that I needed thirty minutes with you. Then I would leave. What do you want me to do?"

Just then, Creek came to our table. "Come with me, Rita. We need to talk." She led Rita to a spot some twenty feet from our table, but I still managed to hear their words. "Rita," Creek said, "we've got a problem. I've got this John Young guy pacing back and forth in the check-in room. If he comes in, are we going to have a fight between the two of them?" Creek stepped closer and looked into her eye. "Now listen, Rita. I don't want a fight between the two of them. I don't want the paperwork." I couldn't help but notice how Creek was more concerned about the paperwork than my safety. After some verbal exchange, they agreed that Rita and I would talk for a while and then the other guard would bring John to the visit room.

Creek left, and Rita joined me at the table. Since our time together was limited, I launched into the reasons why I had made a hurried trip to see her. "Rita, your letter sounded so desperate."

Her eyes widened, and she looked surprised. "What are you talking about?" she asked.

"Your letter," I said. "Your letter sounded like a cry for help. You said that your time clock was running down and that you couldn't wait to get off this earth. And you said that someone had threatened you."

After a slight hesitation, Rita spoke. "Yes, time is running short, but I'm not desperate. I was just upset that I haven't read everything you've written. You've just sent me bits and pieces."

"What's the hurry?" I asked. "Are you still considering suicide?"

"That hasn't changed," Rita shot back. "I want to have everything in order. I don't want things left unfinished."

"How much time do we have?"

"Months, just months," Rita answered.

Although her suicide threats were common, I had never known how to respond. If John had not been waiting, I would have asked if she was really serious about committing suicide and if so, when would it be and what would make Rita change her mind. But I did not have the time.

Time was moving quickly, and I could not help but wonder, *Was John waiting in the parking lot with a loaded gun? After all, Rita told me during an earlier conversation that he can act a little crazy.* "Maybe we had better have John come in," I suggested. "He may be freaking out."

"Yes," Rita answered. "He's probably upset."

"How do you want to handle this?" I asked. "Do you want me to stay or leave?"

"I don't care," she said. "That's up to you."

"Well, what's he going to be like when he comes in? Is he going to be crazy or what?"

Rita shrugged. "I have no idea," she said.

For a few seconds I struggled with my dilemma: should I be concerned about my safety and leave, or should I yield to my writer's curiosity? "I'll stay."

Rita walked to the desk and asked the guard to have John Young sent to the visit room. The guard made the call. We moved to a larger table, and I made certain that an empty chair sat between Rita and me. *No need to get John more upset*, I thought. While trying to add some humor to the situation, I asked whether we should hug when I left or skip that part.

"No, no," Rita said as we both laughed. "We'd better skip that part."

We were still laughing when John walked in but stopped as he approached the table and sat next to Rita. "What took so long?" John asked. His face was flushed, and his dark pupils had widened. John's thirty-minute wait must have seemed endless.

"We asked to have you sent in right away," Rita said. "You know this place. I don't know why it took so long."

"That's right," I added. "We tried to get you in as soon as possible."

Rita's voice was soft and calm and more soothing than I had heard before. John reached into his shirt pocket and handed me his debit card. "Why don't you get us all something to drink?" he asked.

I imagined that this was John's way of getting a private moment with Rita. "Sure," I added. "What does everybody want?" John wanted a Coke, and Rita asked for a Dr. Pepper heated in the microwave.

"Give it two minutes," she said.

While I got the drinks, the two of them whispered to each other. When I returned, I gave John his card and the three of us took sips from our drinks and wondered what we would talk about next. Our small talk was interrupted when John turned to me and said, "I can't understand why you'd want to write a book about Rita." Normally, Rita would have bristled at such a remark, but instead she smiled.

"That's an easy question," I answered. "Rita's had a very interesting but tragic life. Her story is so filled with injustice that it needs to be told. I would hope that someday people will read this book and become very angry that something like this could have happened to Rita. That it could have happened to anyone." John nodded his head in agreement, and Rita smiled.

"I should go and let the two of you talk," I said.

"Don't leave," John said. "I like talking with you."

While surprised, I agreed to stay. John's conversation moved to a discussion about what Rita could eat from the vending machine. Since prisoners were no longer allowed to walk to the vending machines, John and I checked out the machines and told her what was available. After some encouragement by John, she chose a bagel and cream cheese. I was asked to heat it in the microwave.

I stood by the microwave, and the two of them talked. An inmate sat at a table while two church women read from a Bible and prayed with her, six stone-faced inmates waited to talk with their attorneys, and for the first time in nearly three years in a world so different from mine, I laughed.

Although the humor was hard felt, I felt guilty about it, too. In the same way that the sanctity of the church prohibited conversation, prison forbad laughter. But I was wrong. Even in an imprisoned society, hope spreads through prayer, the occasional laugh, a witty joke, or a wisecrack or two. And without hope, death becomes an option.

I returned to the table. John and I shook hands. I told Rita goodbye; we didn't hug.

Rita, with a slight smile on her face, later told me that word of my visit moved through her prison wing like an August grass fire. Inmates and guards talked about the day when Rita had two male visitors at the same time: two men, loaded with testosterone, ready to hit and kick and roll on the prison floor. But through Rita's control, the three of us sat in the visit room, talking and visiting like long-lost friends. She became known as "the player."

Since that day, when John Young and I went face to face, we have talked on several occasions. I have found him to be one of Rita's best friends and her staunchest supporter, always looking to help me in my pursuit of her story. He is not the evil man I had once feared.

23 Pieces of Floating Cork

Her initial plea, "You're the only one who has listened to my story," had hooked me and then shadowed me for the next two and a half years. Not a single day slipped by without my giving her a thought. Rita never asked for money or pity or the right to censor my work. She asked only that I tell the truth. But truth, as I soon discovered, appeared in bits and pieces and flashed like fireflies in the night. Truth was an illusion, or so I thought, and life without truth was one without structure. I saw life without truth in the criminal world, the judicial system, and our politicians and governmental leaders, who called it spin.

Rita's tragedy was shaped by social and judicial inequities and a host of bad choices. An abusive childhood, lack of a good role model, and a string of bad relationships pushed her into a life surrounded by people who sang the same songs. Hers was a hellish way of life but the only one she knew. If the state had examined the crime scene after May 6, 1988, when Betty Boyer told her story, and found even a strand of hair, a drop of blood, or a piece of human tissue, the alleged beating might have fit within the realm of possibility. But without forensic evidence, the jury was left to take the word of the state's only eyewitness, who was shifty at best. Logic, compassion, and a willingness to look for the truth were needed, but someone had to care. And that was the crux of Rita's problem: no one cared. To the prosecution and others who looked from a distance, she was *poor white trash*.

When I allowed myself, even for a moment, to believe that Rita was innocent and would be jailed for life, I gave way to depression. Grief wore me down; my body slowed. But an unspoken promise or perhaps a spiritual prodding stirred me into a stubborn search for the truth. I read some five thousand pages from the transcripts of Richard's 1988 trial and a second trial held ten years later. I looked for new information; I wrestled with troubled testimony. But confusion grew like field grass.

During Richard's trial, Garnati called Danny Walker, a seventeen-year-old, unemployed high school dropout, to the stand. Walker testified that he attended a party of eight to ten people at the Nitz trailer in mid-April 1988. At about one thirty a.m., according to Walker, Rita took the last stragglers home, leaving Richard and Walker alone at the trailer. Between deep pulls from his cigarette, Richard told Walker that he killed a faggot. It happened in the Grassy Bottoms, Walker explained. Richard drove slowly, and another car crawled close behind. Both cars stopped. The man in the second car, later identified as Michael Miley, approached Richard's car and propositioned him. Richard drew a twenty-two-caliber handgun, shot Miley in the forehead, decapitated him, and loaded his headless body into the trunk of the victim's car. Later Richard buried the head and gun and drove to the trailer, where he told Rita to drive one of their cars and follow him to Rocky Comfort.

Walker said that Richard boasted about the killing and wanted to show him the body. The two left in Walker's pickup truck, and as they reached the top of a hill that led into Rocky Comfort, they saw two police officers hovering around a 1972 Chevrolet.

"They found him," Richard said.

Walker backed down the hill, and they sped away.

Mike Stearns, another state witness at Richard's trial, testified that Richard told him about killing a gay man. Stearns and Richard were drinking beer at the Hideaway Lounge, a tavern behind Peterson's Plumbing in Carbondale. Richard told Stearns about a homosexual man who followed him home and how it pissed him off. "I blew him away," Richard reportedly told Stearns. Richard said that he went inside the trailer, got a gun, came back out, and shot Miley and cut his head off. "Richard said 'We got rid of the body' but didn't say who 'we' was."

Richard Nitz had testified that Danny Walker killed Michael Miley and gave him Miley's credit cards for work Richard had done on Walker's car. Neither Richard's nor Rita's fingerprints were found on any evidence discovered in the garage; the state took no fingerprints, hair, or blood standards from Danny Walker, even though the court was told that Walker was known to have chased a few gay men with a baseball bat.

And there is Steven and Kathy Gilbert's recorded transcript—a story the jury never heard—in which Dickie Waide asked his mother for an alibi for the nights of April 6, 7, and 8, 1988. The transcript revealed a pattern of harassment by Richard Nitz, Waide, and Walker, a discussion of Michael Miley's credit cards, and references to the location of the missing head. The police never interviewed the Gilberts, and I can only wonder whether all the facts were known.

I am puzzled by the lack of testimony from Walker, Stearns, and the Gilberts at Rita's trial. At the very least, their stories would have cast doubt on Boyer's testimony. Rita later told me that since Richard had been found guilty, Drew wanted to use a different defense and rely on the inconsistencies of Betty Boyer's story; and Drew was afraid that Garnati would twist Stearns's and Walker's arms, increasing the chance that they would implicate her.

Larry Beard and J. R. Moore told me about a newspaper article that described a murder committed by Betty Boyer's brother several years after the death of Michael Miley. The victim, like Miley, was shot, decapitated, and placed in his car trunk before the car was set on fire. The brother is serving natural life for first-degree murder. At one time the police thought Betty Boyer might have been involved in Miley's death. Larry Beard and Rita Nitz had expressed similar views.

What about Betty Boyer's husband, Charles Hooker? "He would kill all the gays if he could" was taken from interview notes written by private investigator Ronald Roach on August 23, 1988. On several occasions, according to Roach, Hooker shook violently and cried. Hooker was concerned about Boyer's safety and said that she left a suicide note on their trailer wall. The intensity of the interview was felt as I read on. "When Hooker was six years old, his father brought a gay to his residence and stood and watched while the gay molested him." Still Hooker said he did not kill Miley. Roach added a few additional thoughts. "I also talked with Charles later at the Gateway Truck Stop and went over the above statements. Mr. Hooker stated the same as above. Mr. Hooker was so nervous that he could not hold onto a cup of coffee."

Bob Burns testified that on the day the police searched Rita and Richard's home, Rita told officers that Glen Murphy boasted about killing a man in the Grassy Bottoms and doing something to conceal the victim's identify.

Plenty of men had motives. Several, it appeared, had veins of hatred that ran through their souls, shedding paths of evil unseen by the unseeing. Hate was like a virus passed from one to another, allowing them to unleash an undeserved anger onto the male homosexual community and, finally, onto Michael Miley.

What if the crime did not take place as Betty Boyer had testified? What if the scene at the trailer, in which she claimed to have seen Richard Nitz batter Miley with a baseball bat, never happened? What do we know for sure?

Betty Boyer claimed at Rita's trial that Richard hit Miley in the head six to eight times (and at Richard's trial, ten to twelve times) with a baseball bat and still, according to the pathologist, no marks were left on the neck, shoulders, or anywhere else on the body. To believe such a claim, each downward swing had to have been an exact hit to the head, with no glancing or direct blows to the rest of the body. No traces of blood, bone, or human tissue were found on the concrete slab where the body fell, on the varnish-free wooden baseball bat used to beat Miley, or on the knife found in Richard and Rita's garage. To believe such a claim, all evidence had to have been washed away by an April rain.

A neighbor testified at Richard's trial that no noise roused him as he slept in his trailer just one hundred feet from where the beating occurred. To believe such a claim, the noise from the verbal altercation and beating, which lasted twenty to forty-five minutes, was muffled by the quiet night. Danny Walker and Mike Stearns testified at Richard's trial that Richard confessed to shooting and decapitating Miley but said nothing about the use of a baseball bat. To believe Boyer's story, Walker's and Stearns's testimony had to be untrue. And finally, Ed Heischmidt, an expert witness for the defense, testified that it was physically impossible for Boyer to see what she claimed to have seen at the trailer on April 6, 1988, and Boyer testified that her vision without glasses was fuzzy at best.

If Betty Boyer's testimony is discounted, we are left with no eyewitness, no forensic evidence, and the testimony of Barbara Winkler, a jailhouse informant, who claimed that Rita confessed to the murder of Miley some twenty times a day at the Williamson County Jail. We are left with maybes. Maybe Richard killed Michael Miley, maybe another party or parties helped him, maybe Rita knew more than she said, and maybe she knew nothing at all.

Each time I looked into the murder of Michael Miley, I was drawn to familiar names: Richard Nitz, Rita Nitz, Betty Boyer, Danny Walker, Dickie Waide, Glen Murphy, Earlene Young, Charles Hooker, and finally, Betty Boyer's brother. Their involvement might have been friendships they shared, material information, or maybe nothing at all. Still they surfaced like pieces of floating cork.

It was another day, another trip to the Dwight Correctional Center, when I shared each theory with Rita. I could not shake the idea that some party or parties may have helped Richard in the murder of Michael Miley. Rita said that she never doubted whether Richard could have shot Miley. "He's capable of killing someone," she said. "But I can't believe he decapitated Miley."

"Why do you say that?" I asked.

She talked about Richard hunting deer with his male friends. "Richard shot the deer, but he wouldn't gut them."

"That's interesting," I said.

"Richard said that when he tried to cut up the deer, he had flashbacks from his Vietnam days. Each time they killed a deer and brought it to our place, Richard came inside while his friends did the cutting. I just don't see how Richard could have cut someone's head off. Richard's friends were farmers and had butchered animals before. They knew how to do it."

Rita and I talked about the strength needed to cut through muscle and the technique needed to cut between vertebrae. We imagined how you would have to lay the head on a hard surface or in your lap while sawing back and forth with a sharp knife. But the autopsy report stated that the cut was clean and did not reveal a sawing motion. The more we talked about it, the more difficult it seemed and the more likely that some acquired skill learned through butchering farm animals would have been helpful. Otherwise the neck would have been mutilated.

"No, I don't think Richard could have done that," Rita said.

Days later I asked a pathologist how one would go about decapitating a human body. After I explained that I was doing research for a book, he began to talk. He explained that the most efficient way would be to cut through the soft tissue at the front of the neck. That would be fairly easy with a sharp knife. But cutting through the bone of the spinal column would be impossible without a saw. If someone were using a knife, he would have to cut in the small spaces between the bone and a good deal of strength would be required. If he tried to saw through with a knife and did not attend to what he was doing, he would have quite a mess. I asked him whether any skill was necessary to do the job, and he answered no. Still, he added, some experience in butchering animals would help.

24 Left in Chains

A month passed, and another, since I had last seen Rita. Now, with a glass wall between us, she looked through strands of hair while her head hung down and her face was drawn with shame. Chains were wrapped around her ankles, handcuffs cut into her arms, and her body leaned forward. As she sat on a metal stool and held a phone to her ear, her words were faint, as though we were communicating through bean cans connected with string.

Rita had written to me, asking that I not come to see her while she was in segregation, but I had not received her letter. In the waiting room, a guard said that our time would be cut from four hours to one and it would be a noncontact visit with a glass wall between us. When I asked why she was in segregation, the guard said that Rita should be the one to tell.

Segregation was difficult, especially if a prisoner did not like her cell mate. Two inmates spent twenty-three hours each day locked in a small cell with two bunk beds, a lavatory, and a steel commode. Privacy was a memory. Inmates were let out one hour each day for exercise.

Now, as I sat on a stool, moving the phone from one ear to the other, I imagined that the prison officials wanted our visit to be difficult. Why else would we have phones that barely worked and look like two children serving detention?

"It was just a misunderstanding," Rita said. "I was tutoring a GED student who was having difficulty grasping the high school math. She was really down. I told her that everybody had trouble with math and that I even did the books for some of the guards. A supervisor overheard part of our conversation and reported me." Rita paused and readjusted her phone. "She didn't understand what I said or she wouldn't have written me up. When I worked in the garment factory, I kept the books. That's what I was talking about." Rita shook her head in disbelief. "I was just trying to build her confidence."

"That's all there was to it?" I asked.

"Yes, that's it," Rita answered.

Inmates were continually pushed down. I was not surprised by her story. "How long will this last?" I asked.

"They have thirty days to complete an investigation," she said. "I've been here for twenty, so I've got another ten."

She asked what was going on and whether I had seen anyone involved in her case. I had continued talking with people, hoping to find a clue or new direction that would lead to the truth. Weeks earlier I talked with Mike Wright and Paul Hyler, both friends of Richard. Although I wanted to share my conversations with Rita, I did not want to upset her, especially while she was in segregation. Wright, a Baptist minister, had worked in an auto body shop with Richard in 1987. While they were good friends, their social interaction centered on watching Wright's children play and having coffee at the local Denny's restaurant with Paul Hyler, Roy Dulaney, and Rita.

"I just can't believe he killed Miley," Wright told me during a telephone conversation. "He could not have done it alone. He's not put together that way. Maybe if he was with some of his younger friends and they had been drinking. Richard liked to get together with the younger guys. It gave him a chance to be in charge and show off a bit."

Wright said that he had talked with Richard several years ago, hoping to get his spiritual life in order. "I told him that he needed to tell the truth, he needed to set the record straight. Richard swore to me that he didn't have anything to do with the murder of Michael Miley. That's what he said, but I don't know whether it's true."

According to Wright, Rita pushed Richard's buttons and made him jealous. "I refused to marry them," Wright said. "They were not a good mix."

Paul Hyler shared similar feelings. I found Hyler working the graveyard shift at a local cab company, where he had been employed since 1977. I showed up at six thirty a.m., introduced myself, and asked whether we could have breakfast together. We went to the same Denny's restaurant the group had frequented fourteen years before. At age sixty-eight, Hyler was eighteen years older than Richard and twenty-eight years older than Rita. Wrinkles were chiseled into his face, and long gray hair grew down his neck. Each time he took a drag from his cigarette, it disappeared as it slid into a spot once occupied by teeth, only to reappear when he exhaled. Years of smoking, drinking, and hard living had demanded a high price from Hyler.

Now, as I faced Rita, I decided to say what was on my mind. "I talked with Mike Wright and Paul Hyler. They brought up some information I hadn't heard before. I'd like to talk with you about it, but I don't want to upset you."

"Go ahead," Rita said, switching the phone from one ear to the other. "Tell me what a bad person I am."

"No," I said. "I'm not going to do that. They just believed that you wore the pants in the family and were always pressing Richard's hot buttons." I leaned back, wondering how she would react. A few thoughtful seconds passed.

"I guess I can see how they might say that," she said. "There were times when I got on Richard pretty good." She bristled. "But that was after he had been gone for a couple of days and I didn't know where he was at. I'd be upset and, sure, I'd press his buttons."

"Paul said that you were always flirting with men," I said. "You tried to make Richard jealous."

"Are we talking about old man Paul?" Rita asked.

"Well, he's sixty-eight, so I guess he'd been fifty-four when you were twenty-nine."

"Yes, that's him," she said. "Old man Paul."

"Paul told me about a time when you, he, and Richard sat in the living room of your trailer. According to Paul, you wore a very skimpy wraparound and he didn't have to look very hard to see your crotch. He said that it made the hair stand up on the back of his neck."

"Oh come on," she said. "You saw Paul. Give me a break."

I laughed. "Well, you do have a point."

A guard told us to end our visit. The hour had passed quickly. Rita asked me to write, and then she looked down, showing the humiliation of being drenched in chains. I nodded and raised my hand, signifying a partial wave, and walked to the first set of sliding glass doors, waiting for the clicking sound that announced my entrance into freedom. Staring into the glass, I saw the reflected image: an aging man with heavy eyes. A man who gave it his best but could have done better. He was surrounded by shapes, movements, and sounds of inmates, visitors, and prison guards. To his back and out of view was Rita, waiting to be led back to her cell.

This man, the one with heavy eyes, thought about the feelings Rita must endure. She will never return to southern Illinois and pick strawberries in May, redecorate a house or select curtains for a picture window, visit with friends at the Mélange coffee shop or stop by Arnold's Market for a gallon of milk. She will never walk her dog through campus woods or attend the funeral of a friend, make love with a tender man or have breakfast at Harbaugh's. All of these freedoms are denied, if one is to believe the prosecution, for silently watching Richard Nitz, a man whom Rita feared, hit Michael Miley with a baseball bat and, on Richard's command, helping load the body into the trunk of a car.

Click. The sliding glass door opened to a hallway that led to the final set of doors. Still staring at me was the tired man, the one with heavy eyes, who had carried his own set of chains since childhood.

Click. The door slid open, and I walked to my locker, removed my wallet and keys, and went to my pickup parked some two hundred yards away. I crawled into my truck, cranked up the engine, and turned onto Highway 47. I turned off the radio and drove in silence. Rita walked back to her six-by-nine-foot cell.

August 2003. For Rita, change moves slowly. After fifteen years of incarceration as Rita Nitz, the Illinois Department of Corrections now calls her Rita J. Brookmyer. She changed her name, prays each day, and fights her past.

Michael Miley's body lies at rest in a small-town cemetery. A tombstone marks his grave. His missing head, possibly buried within a few miles of Progress Cemetery, stirs sadness for family and friends. But for Rita, the head offers hope. For if it is found and shows no evidence of a beating, Betty Boyer, the state's only eyewitness, would be proved wrong.

Rita and Richard continue their separate appeals. After Richard was convicted of the murder of Michael Miley and sentenced to death, he filed an appeal, claiming that he was on medication while housed in the Williamson County Jail and did not receive a hearing to determine whether he was fit to stand trial. On June 21, 1996, the Illinois Supreme Court ruled 4-3 that because Richard was taking Tranzene, a psychotropic drug, during his trial, he should have had a fitness hearing to determine whether the drug rendered him incapable of assisting with his own defense. He was granted a second trial, was convicted of first-degree murder once again, and was sentenced to life in prison.

In 1998 Richard Nitz filed an appeal, saying that it was unconstitutional for the judge to have issued a life-without-parole sentence. His attorney maintained that such a sentence had to come from the jury, not the judge. The Illinois Supreme Court heard Richard's appeal and reduced his sentence to sixty years, allowing parole in thirty years for good behavior.

Six years later, in March 2004, Richard received a judicial setback. The Fifth District Appellate Court reversed its earlier decision and reinstated a life sentence for Richard Nitz.

"Mr. Nitz, has been, in my opinion, the luckiest murderer in Illinois history," Williamson County state's attorney Charles Garnati said. "But today, his luck just ran out and he will serve the rest of his life in prison."

On November 18, 2004, less than a year later, the Fifth District Appellate Court reversed its earlier decision and reduced Richard's sentence to sixty years. Since Richard was originally sentenced in 1988, the truth-in-sentencing laws do not apply. Richard can serve half the term with good behavior, leaving him eligible for parole in 2018. On hearing the decision, Garnati pledged to continue the fight to keep Richard Nitz in prison for the rest of his life. Richard, convicted of murder and the decapitation of Michael Miley, had moved from a sentence of death to life without parole, to sixty years, to life without parole again, and back to sixty years with eligibility for parole in thirty. With fifteen served, he might be paroled in another fifteen years.

Rita's appeal process has been quite different. She too filed an appeal, claiming that she was on Tranzene while housed in the Williamson County Jail and did not receive a hearing to determine whether she was fit to stand trial. Her appeal was denied.

Rita filed a second appeal, but the review board ruled that her application had been submitted after the deadline. Garnati said that he was "thrilled" with the decision. "It appears that after twelve long years of legal battles, Rita Nitz will finally spend the rest of her life in prison," he said. "This ruling here pretty much turns the lights out on Rita Nitz."

On September 14, 2004, Rita's appeal was again turned down by the Fifth District Appellate Court. And again, Garnati was happy with the decision. "We've been fighting these appeals the last sixteen years and I'll fight them another sixteen years if I have to."

Peggy Miley, the mother of Michael Miley, was also pleased with the appellate court's decision. "I'm hoping that both of them [Richard and Rita] stay in prison for life," Miley said. "There's a lot more I could say, but I won't because I don't think it would do any good."

Still Rita says we have not read her final chapter. Until the Supreme Court rules otherwise, she clings to the dream that a court will hear her plea and right the injustice that has been done to her. While she waits, hoping to pray herself home, time is cruel. Each night moves slowly and repeats itself like a stale dream.

Epilogue

On March 8, 2004, the *Southern Illinoisan*, the local newspaper in Carbondale, Illinois, published a story about an appellate court's ruling on the case of Richard Nitz. The three appellate court judges—Kuehn, Goldenhersh, and Welch—had no doubt as they wrote their decision. "We believe that a jury would have found, beyond a reasonable doubt, that this murder was accompanied by brutal and heinous behavior indicative of wanton cruelty. The method employed to kill Michael Miley conjures up images of Robert DeNiro's portrayal of Al Capone in the movie, 'The Untouchables.' ... The defendant used a baseball bat to beat Miley to death. Moreover, in an ill-conceived effort to frustrate the identification of Miley's body and thereby escape prosecution, the defendant decapitated Miley. . . . The whereabouts of Miley's head remains unknown to this day. Given our opinion of what the jury would have done had this crime's brutality been submitted to the jury, we find the constitutional failure was harmless. We affirm the trial judge's—Williamson County Circuit Court Judge John Speroni—imposition of a life sentence."

The story has been told so many times that allegations have become facts: Richard Nitz beat Michael Miley unconscious with a baseball bat and, with Rita's help, loaded the body into the trunk of his car. Minutes later, Richard, with Rita standing by his side, shot Michael Miley in the head and decapitated him. While the prosecution portrayed Rita as the loving and supportive wife of Richard Nitz, the defense was unable to place any separation between Rita and Richard. In the jury's eyes, she was like the spare tire mounted under a rusted-out pickup truck. One was never without the other.

Garnati's determination to levy the maximum punishments on Richard and Rita Nitz has been relentless. I can only wonder whether a life sentence for Rita was the result of his unwavering pursuit of justice, the horrific nature of the crime, a vendetta of sorts, political motives, or some reason I will never understand. After all, prisons are filled with people who committed murders and are serving far less time than Rita, a woman who the prosecution admits did not actively participate in the murder of Michael Miley.

December 2004. I met with Rita at the Dwight Correctional Center. The visit room was filled with holiday visitors, and the air still reeked of buttered popcorn. Time was running out; this was Rita's last chance to tell her story.

"Your book is nearing publication," I said. "If I'm going to make any change, it has to be done now. Is there anything that you would like to tell me? Anything that would help explain how Michael Miley died?"

Seconds passed as she looked down. "No, not that I can think of. I wasn't there, so I don't know what happened."

"You've told me before that Betty Boyer might have been at the crime scene," I said. "Tell me exactly what Betty said to you."

"Betty said that they had been partying and things got crazy. Things got out of hand."

"Be more precise," I said. "Who was at the party, and how did things go crazy?"

"Betty didn't say who *they* was. I assumed it was Betty, Richard, and his friends. And she didn't say what went wrong. That's all I know."

"Sometimes you talk in riddles," I said.

"Sometimes I talk in metaphors," she answered with a smile.

I was frustrated and puzzled as to why Rita seemed to hold back when Betty Boyer was implicated in the crime. *Why would she protect Betty,* I thought. *Betty's testimony drove the stake into Rita's heart. And what about Richard?* When I said that his latest prison photo showed a man stressed to the limit, someone ready to crack, she said that she hoped he was okay.

"Show me your anger. Why don't you nail Betty and Richard? They're responsible for you spending the rest of your life in prison."

"That's not who I am. That's not what I'm about."

"According to the pathologist's report, dirt, grass, and crushed leaves were found in Miley's pubic hair. How would that fit into this scenario?"

"Maybe somebody made Miley take down his pants and do something. Richard loved to humiliate people."

"So what we have is a theory that there was a party, probably with drugs and alcohol, where Michael Miley somehow became the object of humiliation and things just went crazy." Rita nodded, seeming to agree with my speculation.

After three years of research and reflection, I still have doubts about what happened that chilly evening of April 6, 1988. The pathologist could not determine the cause of death; no marks were on the body, leaving one to wonder how a beating could have occurred. No blood or human tissue was found on the alleged weapon, on the baseball bat, or at the alleged crime scene, Rita's trailer. Not one shred of forensic evidence tied her to the crime. Only the testimony of Betty Boyer, a questionable witness whose objective was to avoid prosecution and maintain the custody of her children, brought Rita down. After all is said and done, I am left, at the very least, with a shadow of doubt, while Rita lives out a life without parole.

Appendix
Sources

Appendix: Inmate Status of Rita and Richard Nitz

Data for both Rita J. Brookmyer Nitz and Richard C. Nitz from the Illinois Department of Corrections (www.idoc.state.il.us), Internet inmate status as of December 6, 2004.

N97463—Brookmyer, Rita J.

Parent Institution:	Dwight Correctional Center
Inmate Status:	In custody
Location:	Dwight
Discharge Reason:	

Vitals

Date of birth:	02-24-1959
Weight:	150 lbs.
Hair:	Brown
Sex:	Female
Height:	5 ft. 04 in.
Race:	White
Eyes:	Blue

Marks, Scars, and Tattoos

Tattoo, arm, left
Pierced ears
Mole, nose

Admission/Release/Discharge Info

Custody Date:	11/08/1989
Projected Parole Date:	Life
Paroled Date:	—
Tentative Discharge Date:	
Discharge from Parole:	Life

Sentencing Information

Mittimus:	89CF55
Class:	M
Count:	3
Offense:	Murder/intent to kill/injure
Custody Date:	05/09/1988
Sentence:	Life

County: Massac
Sentence Discharged?: No

A11030—Nitz, Richard C.

Parent Institution: Menard Correctional Center
Inmate Status: In custody
Location: Menard
Discharge Reason:

Vitals

Date of Birth: 10-25-1952
Weight: 160 lbs.
Hair: Brown
Sex: Male
Height: 5 ft. 09 in.
Race: White
Eyes: Green

Marks, Scars, and Tattoos

Tattoo, arm, left—heart
Tattoo, arm, right—banner, "MM"
Tattoo, shoulder, left—"Jake," peace sign
Tattoo, finger(s), left hand—"Love"

Admission/Release/Discharge Info

Custody Date: 07/30/1998
Projected Parole Date: 05/09/2018
Paroled Date:
Tentative Discharge Date:
Discharge from Parole: 05/09/2021

Sentencing Information

Mittimus: 88CF162
Class: M
Count: 2
Offense: Murder/intent to kill/injure
Custody Date: 5/09/1988
Sentence: 60 years 0 months 0 days

County:	Williamson
Sentence Discharged?:	No

Mittimus:	88CF162
Class:	M
Count:	2
Offense:	Murder/intent to kill/injure
Custody date:	05/02/1988
Sentence:	Death
County:	Williamson
Sentence Discharged:	Yes

Mittimus:	85CF8
Class:	4
Count:	1
Offense:	Bad check/>$150 or 2nd offense
Custody Date:	04/24/1985
Sentence:	3 years 0 months 0 days
County:	Perry
Sentence Discharged:	Yes

Mittimus:	79CF112
Class:	4
Count:	1
Offense:	Carry/possess firearm/2nd and subq
Custody date:	12/19/1979
Sentence:	3 years 0 months 0 days
County:	Jackson
Sentence discharged:	Yes

Mittimus:	79CF94
Class:	3
Count:	1
Offense:	Theft >$300–$10K
Custody Date:	06/28/1979
Sentenced:	4 years 0 months 0 days
County:	Williamson
Sentence Discharged:	Yes

Mittimus:	79CF94
Class:	2
Count:	1
Offense:	Burglary
Custody Date:	06/28/1979
Sentence:	4 years 0 months 0 days
County:	Williamson
Sentence Discharged:	Yes

Mittimus:	75CF295
Class:	2
Count:	1
Offense:	Burglary
Custody Date:	06/11/1975
Sentence:	3 years 0 months 0 days
County:	Rock Island
Sentence Discharged:	Yes

Sources

Abbott, Jack Henry. *In the Belly of the Beast: Letters from Prison.* New York: Vintage, 1981.

Cole, Dana K. "Psychodrama and the Training of Trial Lawyers: Finding the Story." 2001. *Association of American Law Schools Web site.* Conference on New Ideas for Experience Teachers: We Teach but Do They Learn? June 9–13, 2001. <www.aals.org/profdev/newideas/cole.pdf>.

Conover, Ted. *Newjack: Guarding Sing Sing.* New York: Vintage, 2001.

Curriden, Mark. "The Informant Trap: Secret Threat to Justice." *National Law Journal* (February 20, 1995).

Dodge, L. Mara. *Whores and Thieves of the Worst Kind: A Study of Women, Crime, and Prisons, 1835–2000.* De Kalb: Northern Illinois UP, 2002.

Exner, Raquel. "Blood on the Carpet: Dad's Shocking Discovery." *Edmonton Sun.*

Franklin, Karen. Interview related to "Assault on Gay America." *Frontline. PBS Web site.* February 15, 2000. <www.pbs.org/wgbh/pages/frontline/shows/assault/interviews/franklin.html>.

Garvey, Ed. "Prisons Are State's Unwise Immoral Growth." *Capital Times* August 7, 2001.

"Finding and Selling Your Story in the Courtroom." *The Synchronics Group Web site.* <www.synchronicsgroup.com/articles/articles_findingcrtroom.htm>.

Gorrell, John. "Bribing for Testimony: Growing Reliance on the Snitch." Editorial. *Washington Free Press.* <www.washingtonfreepress.org/46>.

Ingerman, Sandra. *Soul Retrieval: Mending the Fragmented Self Through Shamanic Practice.* San Francisco: HarperSanFrancisco, 1991.

Jacobson, Neil S., and John M. Gottman. *When Men Batter Women: New Insights into Ending Abusive Relationships.* New York: Simon and Schuster, 1998.

Marshall, Lawrence. "The Snitch System." *Northwestern University School of Law Web site.* Center for Wrongful Convictions. <www.law.northwestern.edu/faculty/clinic/Marshall/Marshall.html>.

"Massachusetts Woman Killed in Domestic Dispute." *All Things Considered.* Natl. Public Radio. December 20, 1993.

Osborne, Thomas Mott. *Within Prison Walls; Being a Narrative of Personal Experience During a Week of Voluntary Confinement in the State Prison at Auburn, New York.* 1914. Montclair, NJ: Patterson Smith, 1969.

Pennington, Nancy, and Reid Hastie. "A Cognitive Theory of Juror Decision Making: The Story Model." *Cardoza Law Review* 13 (1991): 519–57.

State of Illinois v. Richard Nitz. No. 88-CF-162. Williamson County, Ill., Circuit Ct. 1988.

State of Illinois v. Richard Nitz. No. 88-CF-162. Supreme Ct. of Ill. 1996.

State of Illinois v. Rita Nitz. No. 89-CF-55. Massac County, Ill., Circuit Ct. 1989.

Trott, Stephen S. "Words of Warning for Prosecutors Using Criminals as Witnessess." *Hastings Law Journal* 47 (1996).

Zimbardo, Philip G. "Stanford Prison Experiment: A Simulation Study of the Psychology of Imprisonment Conducted at Stanford University." *Stanford Prison Experiment Web site.* 1999–2005. <www.prisonexp.org.>

Larry L. Franklin grew up in Illinois and received a bachelor of science degree from the University of Illinois, a master of music degree from Southern Illinois University, and a master of fine arts degree in creative nonfiction from Goucher College in Baltimore, Maryland.